Microsoft CRM 4.0 User Handbook

Stamati Crook
stamati.crook@redware.com

redware research ltd
104 Tamworth Road, Hove, BN3 5FH, England.
web http://www.redware.com email sync@redware.com telephone 0845 3010 444

Microsoft CRM 4.0 User Handbook
by Stamati Crook

Copyright © Stamati Crook 2007, 2008.

Published by redware research limited.

All rights reserved. The book is copyright and no part shall be reproduced, stored in a retrieval system, or transferred by any means: electronic, mechanical, photocopying, recording, or otherwise without written permission from the publisher. No patent liability is assumed with respect to the use of the information contained herein.

The information in this book is distributed on an "as is" basis. Although every precaution has been taken in the preparation of this handbook, the publisher and author assume no responsibility for errors or omissions. Neither is any liability assumed for damages caused or alleged to be caused directly or indirectly from the use of the information contained herein.

Trademarked names may appear in this book. Rather than use a trademark symbol with every occurrence of a trademarked name, we use the names only in an editorial fashion and to the benefit of the trademark owner with no intention of infringement of the trademark.

For information, please contact:

>**redware research ltd**.
>104 Tamworth Road, Hove BN3 5FH, England.
>http://www.redware.com
>sync@redware.com
>**0845 3010 444**
>**+44 (0) 203 179 9444**

ISBN 978-0-9556859-0-3

To Victor and James for being the only guys left to talk tech with and Marge for helping me out with CRM.

1. Contents

1. Contents	3
2. Introduction	6
3. Features	7
3.1. Activities	7
3.2. Microsoft Outlook Integration	7
3.3. Customisation	8
3.4. Programming	8
3.5. Security	8
3.6. Issues	8
3.7. Competitors	10
4. Software	11
4.1. Client Software	11
4.2. Server Software	11
4.3. Hosted CRM	11
4.4. CRM Live	12
4.5. External Connector	12
4.6. Other Software	12
4.7. Security	13
4.8. Virtual PC	13
5. Using CRM	15
5.1. Views	16
5.2. Forms	17
5.3. Notes and Attachments	20
5.4. Advanced Find	20
5.5. Exporting CRM data to Excel	21
5.6. Mail Merge to Word	22
5.7. Word Templates	23
5.8. Email	23
5.9. Email Templates	24
5.10. Send Direct Email	25
5.11. Quick Campaigns	26
5.12. Sharing and Assignment	27
6. Customers	29
6.1. Accounts	29
6.2. Contacts	29
6.3. Relationship Roles	30
7. Activities	31
7.1. Tasks	33
7.2. Email	33
7.3. Fax	33
7.4. Phone Call	33
7.5. Letter	33
7.6. Appointment	33
7.7. Service Activity	35
7.8. Campaign Response	35
8. Outlook Client	36
8.1. Tracking Contacts	37

- 8.2. Mail Merge in Outlook 39
- 8.3. Tasks 39
- 8.4. CRM Options 40
- 8.5. Email Synchronisation 41
- 8.6. Tracking and Synchronisation Options 42
- 8.7. Laptop Client Synchronisation 43
- 8.8. Diagnostic Tool 43
9. Workplace 45
    - 9.1. Calendar 45
    - 9.2. Queues 46
    - 9.3. Announcements 47
    - 9.4. Personalise Workplace 47
10. Products 49
    - 10.1. Unit Groups and Items 49
    - 10.2. Price List Items 50
    - 10.3. Discount Lists 50
11. Sales 52
    - 11.1. Leads 53
    - 11.2. Opportunities 54
    - 11.3. Quotations 56
    - 11.4. Orders 59
    - 11.5. Invoices 60
    - 11.6. Currency 60
    - 11.7. Sales Administration 60
    - 11.8. Sales Pipeline 60
    - 11.9. Sales Quotas 61
12. Marketing 62
    - 12.1. Marketing Lists 62
    - 12.2. Campaigns 63
    - 12.3. Campaign Activities 64
    - 12.4. Distribute Campaign Activities via Mail Merge (Outlook) 66
    - 12.5. Campaign Templates 66
    - 12.6. Campaign Responses 66
13. Service 69
    - 13.1. Cases 69
    - 13.2. Contract Template 71
    - 13.3. Contract 72
    - 13.4. Knowledge Base 73
14. Scheduling 75
    - 14.1. Resources and Equipment 75
    - 14.2. Service Type 76
    - 14.3. Scheduling an Activity 79
    - 14.4. Preferred Resources 80
    - 14.5. Service Calendar 81
    - 14.6. Business Closures 82
15. Reports 83
    - 15.1. Report Viewer 83
    - 15.2. Report Wizard 84
    - 15.3. Running Reports 87
    - 15.4. Scheduling Reports 88

	15.5.	SQL Server Reporting Services	88
16.	Workflow		89
	16.1.	Workflow Triggers	89
	16.2.	Workflow Steps	90
	16.3.	Dynamic Values	90
	16.4.	Workflow Conditions	91
	16.5.	Wait Conditions	91
	16.6.	Sales Pipeline Phases	92
17.	Security		95
	17.1.	Business Unit	95
	17.2.	Users	96
	17.3.	Security Roles	98
	17.4.	Teams	99
18.	Customisation		100
	18.1.	Views	100
	18.2.	Preview Form	101
	18.3.	Entities	101
	18.4.	Attributes	102
	18.5.	Forms	104
	18.6.	JavaScript	104
	18.7.	Iframes	105
	18.8.	Relationships	105
	18.9.	Renaming an Entity Description	107
	18.10.	Relationship Roles	107
19.	Data Management		109
	19.1.	Export and Import from Excel	109
	19.2.	Bulk Import	109
	19.3.	Duplicate Detection	110
	19.4.	Data Migration Manager	111
	19.5.	Third Party Software	111
20.	Resources		112
	20.1.	Redware Research Limited	112
	20.2.	Recommended Books	112
	20.3.	Internet and Blogs	112
	20.4.	Microsoft Training	112
	20.5.	Third Party Software	112
21.	Index		114
22.	redware research limited		117

2. Introduction

The Microsoft CRM 4.0 User Handbook is for people using and evaluating Microsoft CRM. A lot of ground is covered with an emphasis on providing a full and concise summary of all the features of CRM rather than a step-by-step guide.

Customer Relationship Management (CRM) software can be configured to influence and monitor many of the communication processes that your business has with its customers. This handbook helps you explore all the functionality that Microsoft CRM offers you as a user.

You will understand the sales cycle, how to run a marketing campaign, and how to schedule appointments and service activities. The user interface is explored in full, both from a web browser and from the Outlook client for CRM, and you will learn how to run a mail merge to Word and export to Excel.

Customisation and workflow features are covered from a user point of view and we do not discuss installation or programming issues (although the author is a programmer). We recommend that you purchase **Working with Dynamics CRM 4.0** by Mike Snyder and Jim Steger if you need to begin extending CRM beyond what is possible with the user interface.

This document provides you with a comprehensive look at Microsoft CRM 4.0 and can be supplemented with books covering CRM 3.0 which are still relevant. One recommendation would be the **Your working day with Microsoft CRM** document distributed by Microsoft (see resources).

There are many facets of CRM, and we cover most of them here. The book does not need to be read sequentially and you can dip into each chapter as required. You could skip the first two chapters if you are keen just to get started with Microsoft CRM but we encourage you to read the chapters on Using CRM, Customers, and Activities (and Outlook if you are using it) before exploring other areas.

The document you are reading is available online at http://www.redware.com/mscrm/handbook and you will find corrections and additions there. Please register for us to send you details of updates to this book and future publications.

We welcome comments and suggestions by email to stamati.crook@redware.com. Please notify us of any errors or suggestions so that they can be corrected promptly.

3. Features

This section looks at some of the features and benefits of Microsoft CRM 4.0 software. You can skip straight to the chapter on Using CRM if you want to start with practical tips on using the software.

Microsoft has looked at the relatively mature CRM marketplace and focussed on core functionality:

- **Contact Management** for centralised storage of customer communication history.
- **Marketing** for lead generation and progress monitoring of leads until they enter the sales cycle. Marketing can also manage campaigns for lists of existing customers.
- **Sales automation** allowing quotations to be made on products with various different pricelists and the promotion of these through to the final order.
- **Customer support** for tracking cases involving customers who may be on support contracts.
- **Service Scheduling** for scheduling resources for customer related activities such as engineering visits.

3.1. Activities

Activities form the basic unit of workflow and are usually assigned an **owner** responsible for carrying them out.

The Activity Types are:

- **Tasks**.
- **Emails**.
- **Phone Calls**.
- **Faxes**.
- **Letters**.
- **Appointments**.
- **Service Activities**.
- **Campaign Responses**.

Activities are created by a user and attached to a CRM record or created automatically as part of a workflow process. Incoming emails can be created automatically as email activity records within CRM and you can easily convert them to leads, sales opportunities, or customer support cases.

An elaborate **workflow** layer has been implemented to allow sophisticated business processes to be applied to each kind of entity (without programming). A sales enquiry task, for example, could automatically be referred to the appropriate manager if not responded to within 24 hours.

Activities are integrated with the **Task List** and the **Calendar** in **Microsoft Exchange** for enterprise wide resource scheduling. This is a major benefit of Microsoft CRM in comparison with other software.

3.2. Microsoft Outlook Integration

CRM integration with **Exchange** (much improved in CRM 4.0) provides one level of integration with Microsoft Outlook. There is also a plug-in for Outlook which customises the Outlook interface to access the CRM application and control data synchronisation. This is particularly useful for organisations that are already heavy Outlook users, as individual emails, tasks, contacts and appointments can be quickly tracked in CRM. Training costs are also lower if the users are already familiar with Outlook.

The Laptop version of Outlook for CRM installs a series of components allowing the full CRM experience (on a subset of data) to take place away from the office. Full synchronisation of data occurs on rejoining the network and the synchronisation software is clever enough to include system customisations (including programmed plug-ins) which are made available on remote laptops together with the core CRM functionality.

3.3. Customisation

Perhaps the greatest strength of Microsoft CRM is the robustness of the customisation framework which allows an experienced end user to perform additions and changes to the underlying database structure that powers CRM:

- **Views** of the data and search facilities can easily be customised by the end user and data exported into a spreadsheet for simple reporting.
- **Workflow** can be created against each kind of entity to match complex business processes without programming.
- The **report wizard** allows simple reports to be built without programming.
- Sophisticated **security** can be defined around users and business units.
- New **attributes** can be easily defined for entities.
- **Forms** can be modified but only one form is permitted for each entity (which can cause issues in larger organisations where different departments have different views of the data).
- New **entities** can be created and related to existing entities.

3.4. Programming

Microsoft excels in providing developers with access to the internal nuts and bolts of their software applications and CRM is no exception. Organisations with access to programmers can benefit from the following features:

- Control of the end-user experience with **JavaScript** programming on forms.
- Full programmatic access to CRM with the **web services** software development kit for integrating existing applications (and building new ones).
- Access to external web pages within CRM using the **iframe** control on forms.
- Integration of complex **SQL Server Reporting Services** reports into the CRM user interface.
- Programming **plug-ins** to control many user interface and application events to alter the default behaviour of CRM. This behaviour can also be synchronised to the laptop client.
- Read-only access directly into the **database** for integration with a wide range of applications whilst respecting the security permissions of each user.
- **Workflow** can be supplemented with code driven functionality.
- Integration with **Sharepoint**.

3.5. Security

CRM has advanced **security** features based on the **ownership** of each entity occurrence by a user. Security can be defined to allow users to keep data private or share information with their business unit or the organisation as a whole.

CRM 4.0 also introduces the idea of **multi-tenancy**, in which multiple companies (or departments) can have completely independent CRM installations running on the same hardware. This is the basis of the hosted implementation of CRM but can be useful in certain corporate situations.

Note: Each user is licensed to access multiple CRM installations.

3.6. Issues

There are some issues with Microsoft CRM that need to be resolved for a successful implementation. Most of these cause **user adoption** problems particularly if users have already had experience of other CRM or sales software.

Microsoft have put a great deal of effort into integrating Outlook with CRM, and Outlook users will require a relatively small amount of training to be able to track contacts, appointments, emails and tasks in CRM. However, many users of CRM will use the application to the full and need training to understand how the application works.

There are issues with any software package especially one that is designed to assist communication with customers. This section details some of the problems that the author has come across in implementations over the last year or so. Your organisation may encounter a completely different set of problems.

Many issues can be resolved quickly by customisation to remove unwanted fields from the existing forms and by defining new attributes for existing forms. For example, the **company name** field must be entered against a lead even for B2C marketing where the organisation is dealing directly with retail customers and this property may need to be changed before users start using the system.

CRM handles B2B and B2C customer relationships with a virtual **customer** entity which can be either an **account** (company) or **contact**. There are some problems with the lead entity which displays the **full name** of the contact on the hyperlink from related records where most B2B organisations might want the **company name** to be displayed. Another issue occurs here if you change the format of the **full name** after implementation, resulting in inconsistent records (as the field is only set when updating a record). These issues can be fixed programmatically.

The promotion of leads to **opportunities** during the sales cycle is one area of confusion which may require thought and training to overcome. Converting a lead to an opportunity creates a new account and contact occurrence as well as the opportunity record. Many users are confused by having data for a customer potentially stored in many places. Relevant historical information might be stored in any of the lead, opportunity, contact, or company entities and related activities. Other software packages offer a **single view of data** for a prospect or customer and this complexity can cause user adoption issues in the early stages of a CRM implementation.

There can be issues where users need to use **multiple email addresses** to send emails. Outlook is more flexible here than the web client and allows several email accounts to be set up so the sender can have different email identities. Another usability issue is that email templates do not have **attachments** and this type of email needs to be configured with workflow.

Letters can be generated easily from within CRM or the Outlook Client with the **mail merge** facility and the Outlook Client can generate the corresponding **letter** activity to record that the letter was sent. You need to use the Outlook Client if you want to automatically attach the merged document into the notes field of the generated activity.

Workflow also needs careful planning and can cause user adoption issues (although this is not the fault of the software). On the one hand, workflow needs to be prototyped and tested, particularly for business critical tasks, before rolling out the implementation. On the other hand, **complex workflow can bog down user acceptance** and can require considerable training effort.

Contracts can sometimes be difficult to manage because they are made read-only once they have been invoiced. This makes it difficult to modify contract details or add new equipment as line items once the contract is live.

There are also some usability issues with Microsoft CRM, some of which stem from its implementation as a **web client with limited access to the desktop**. For example, the creation of mail merge letters and integration with Word is tighter from the Outlook client than from the web client.

Another example that can slow down an implementation is the impracticality of entering **large product pricelists** via the user interface. At some stage in a complex implementation involving large pricelists you will need to hire programming talent (although clever use of importing might overcome some problems here).

3.7. Competitors

Leaving aside cost implications, any organisation wishing to implement CRM which is already a heavy user of **Microsoft Exchange** and other Microsoft technologies and has access to business analysts to help configure the installation would be well advised to implement Microsoft CRM.

There are several well established competitors providing similar functionality and most are fully featured out-of-the-box and require less customisation effort than Microsoft CRM. A small selection is listed below together with a subjective opinion as to their place in the CRM marketplace:

- **ACT!** is a respectable sales and marketing product for small groups of sales people. It is relatively cheap and requires few resources, and many sales people are already familiar with it. It allows several databases to be defined easily and is good for running individual campaigns. The software cannot cope with large numbers of users, and ACT! is best applied in a sales scenario, perhaps with a team of fewer than 10 persons, or where salespeople work independently on separate databases.
- **Goldmine's** history is similar to that of ACT!, although they implemented a robust database infrastructure some time ago and is better for larger, sales-oriented, businesses (perhaps up to 40 people).
- **Salesforce.com** is moving into the CRM marketplace from sales automation and is very popular in the US as a hosted system with a pay-monthly subscription. Microsoft has specifically designed many of the technical features of CRM 4.0 to compete directly against Salesforce.com.
- Accounting vendors often offer a CRM solution to complement their accounting packages. Sage is one such vendor that is strong in the CRM marketplace with Act! and **Saleslogix** and other packages. However, the fact that both software packages come from the same vendor does not always mean that there is good integration between them.
- **Siebel** (Oracle) and other vendors offer high end CRM implementations. Again Microsoft is specifically addressing high end enterprises with 6,000+ users already possible with Microsoft CRM 3.0.

4. Software

This chapter describes the software components that make up a typical CRM installation. Skip this section and move to the **Using CRM** section if you are keen to get on with looking at CRM functionality.

4.1. Client Software

CRM users can access all CRM functionality either on the local network or over the Internet using just **Internet Explorer**.

Note: Internet Explorer 6/SP2 or Internet Explorer 7 must be used.

The same functionality and user interface can also be accessed from the **Desktop Client for Microsoft Outlook**, which also offers better integration with Microsoft Office and the Windows Desktop. There are also open source and third party applications allowing access to CRM from **Mobile Devices** or within **Microsoft Office**.

The laptop version allows a subset of the data (including customisations) to be synchronised with a special **Laptop Client for Outlook**. The user can go off network, modify local CRM data and synchronise changes back into CRM when they reconnect to the network (only one user can be set up on each machine).

Microsoft has also announced special pricing for user licences that are **read-only** or attached to a specific **device** so that shift workers can use the same PC but consume only one license. **Administrative** users can also be set up (without a licence) to access administrative functions but cannot access CRM data.

4.2. Server Software

Microsoft CRM 4.0 is provided as a web server application which can be implemented **on premise** in different ways:

- CRM **Workgroup** is licensed for up to 5 users.
- CRM **Professional** allows a single CRM installation on one server.
- CRM **Enterprise** allows **multi-tenancy** where several CRM installations can run side by side on the same server and also allows you to share the load on multiple servers if you have a large number of users.

Note: The Standard version of CRM 3.0 has been discontinued, and user licences will be upgraded to the Professional version in certain circumstances.

The server is a **web application** running on Internet Information Services (**IIS**) written in the **.NET Framework 2.0** and utilises a single **SQL Server 2005** database (or one for each CRM tenancy with the Enterprise version). **SQL Server Reporting Services** are used for producing reports integrated with the CRM user interface.

Exchange Server is optional, as the local SMTP server can be used for outgoing mail and the **email router** can be configured either for Exchange or for POP3 email servers or the Outlook Client used to control emails. Workflow is implemented with the **Windows Workflow Foundation** although this is hidden from the average user. **Language packs** are available for over 20 languages to localise the application with different users able to access a different language pack on the same CRM installation.

4.3. Hosted CRM

Microsoft is positioning CRM 4.0 directly against Salesforce.com which has 400,000 users in the USA and has pushed the boat out to ensure that Microsoft CRM 4.0 can operate as a **fully hosted** system supported by a network of hosting resellers. **Multi-tenancy** allows multiple CRM installations to share the same hardware, reducing the costs for the hosting providers.

All the functionality of CRM 3.0 is now supported within the CRM application so that all customisation can be done by an experienced user or analyst using a web browser. Workflow and simple reports can be created without needing to run any software on the server and the database structure can be altered by a user using the web interface or by a programmer using web services over the internet.

Note: Most hosting providers will probably limit functionality in a similar fashion to CRM Live at least for a standard service (see below).

4.4. CRM Live

A Microsoft hosted version of CRM is available in the USA as part of the **CRM Live** service and is available in **standard** and **enterprise** versions. Both versions allow customisation, workflow, reporting (with the wizard), and programmer access to the CRM web services with a minimum of 5 users.

The main restrictions of CRM Live (probably shared with most standard hosted implementations) include the inability to read the database directly and not being able to add programmed plug-ins to alter the default behaviour of the application (although some hosting resellers might provide these features). Reports can only be created with the report wizard and programmers cannot add their own reports to your CRM installation. The ability to run a separate web site and web services on the same domain is also useful for some situations.

The Enterprise version has more storage space and allows the use of the Laptop Outlook Client for CRM which can synchronise remote data for use when not connected to the internet. Programmers should note that the CRM web services are available within the Laptop client for CRM, raising interesting possibilities for integrating data locally onto a laptop and then synchronising with the CRM Live system.

Microsoft has taken care to make it easy to migrate from a hosted solution to an on premise solution if you eventually decide to purchase the software for use on your own network.

The CRM Live service for CRM is not expected outside the USA until early 2009. Microsoft is encouraging partners to offer **on demand** hosted CRM services and many will also be bundling hosted Exchange email.

4.5. External Connector

Microsoft has a special licensing requirement for web sites and external applications that integrate with CRM. You do not need an **external license** if you are using a web site to capture data to add into CRM without showing any existing CRM data to the web site users.

The external connector license is required if customers or agents of the organisation regularly log into the web site and view or update data already entered into CRM. You are not supposed to use the External Connector to allow internal users to connect and update CRM data (unless these users have a valid CRM licence).

Note: Using a read-only licence and importing data manually into CRM via a spreadsheet file could be a workaround with regard to the requirement for an external connector licence.

4.6. Other Software

Microsoft provides additional software:

- **CRM Email Router** to synchronise incoming and outgoing email with CRM automatically (you can also do this with the Outlook Client). Both Exchange and SMTP/POP3 mail server infrastructures are now supported.

- The SDK documents the **web services** and allows you to access CRM data from your own application.
- The SDK also allows you to integrate software modules **as plug-ins** (written in .NET 2.0) directly into the server application.
- The **data migration manager** allows you to migrate thousands of records into CRM efficiently.
- The **integration service** (not seen by the author) allows synchronisation of data between applications to be configured.
- Microsoft also offers integration with **MS Dynamics** accounting packages.

There are some third-party add-ons for Microsoft CRM produced by independent software vendors, some of which are mentioned in the chapter on resources.

Note: *The author sells add-ons for CRM to integrate with text messaging and telephone systems and popular accounting packages in the UK. Please see http://www.redware.com/mscrm for more details.*

4.7. Security

The CRM client is a web-based application which runs on Internet Explorer only and uses **Windows security** for user authentication. You can also set up authentication to allow internet users who do not log onto a VPN to access CRM with a user name and password. Emails are sent using the server (SMTP) email agent, so you can access CRM and send emails from any remote machine.

Note: *You can set up the security on Internet Explorer to always prompt for a username and password to access CRM so you can log on to CRM with a different identity to the currently logged on Windows user.*

4.8. Virtual PC

Virtual PC is an excellent way to evaluate CRM and also develop and test customisations without having to set up a complete development environment. Microsoft ships a Virtual PC version of CRM which can be installed on a machine with 2 GB of RAM and at least 12GB of free disk space.

The Virtual PC installation contains all the software required to carry out development including SQL Server 2005 and Visual Studio 2005. A full copy of Windows Server 2003 runs in a virtual environment on your PC and is also a great way to demonstrate CRM or provide your users with a CRM play area.

Installation is straightforward, but here are some tips to make the best use of Virtual PC:

- Virtual PC has a **host** key which defaults to the **AltGr** button found usually at the lower right of your keyboard next to the **space** bar. Press **host+delete** for the **control+alt+delete** necessary to log on to the server.
- Note that the **Administrator** user has **pass@word1** as the user password and the keyboard is in US format, so you will need **shift+2** for the @ character.
- Press **host+enter** to toggle to full screen and back (you may need to redefine the display settings for this to work).
- You may find that the mouse does not travel outside the Virtual PC window to allow selection of the menu options for the Virtual PC session. This is because mouse pointer integration is not on and you need to press the **host** key so that the mouse can be used to select the menu options.
- Set up the **networking** on the Virtual PC by clicking on the TCP/IP option in your LAN Network Properties and make sure that you have a compatible IP definition with the host machine. Do not choose the same IP address but make the subnet mask and the default gateway (DNS) IP address the same as the host. You should be able to browse the Internet from the Virtual PC.
- It is possible to move files between the real PC environment and the Virtual PC using drag and drop with Windows Explorer on each machine. If this does not work then you might share a drive on the host machine and access it from the Virtual PC with a DOS command, for example

net use z:\192.168.1.100\temp. You will encounter a serious error with the Windows Desktop which can be ignored temporarily while you use a DOS session to copy files as follows – **copy z:*.zip c:\temp*.zip**. Remove the share with the following DOS command: **net use z: /delete**.
- Use the CD-ROM to copy files if you cannot connect with the virtual network or drag and drop. There is a facility to share folders, and this requires that you install the **Virtual Machine Additions** from the menu of a running Virtual PC session (however the author has not managed to get this to work properly.)
- Setting up a new user and remembering passwords can be problematic because of the password policy. Change the **password policy** on the Windows 2003 machine to make things easier. Remember to disable automatic user authentication on the browser so that you can log into CRM with multiple identities.
- Set up a Virtual PC for each site and develop customisations and export the customisations to an XML file which can be installed onto the live CRM installation.
- The **undo disks** setting allows you to revert to the previously saved session if required.

5. Using CRM

Microsoft has done wonders creating a desktop style user interface within a browser environment (although it is Internet Explorer only).

The top right of the page indicates the currently logged on **user details** with the left hand **navigation pane** allowing navigation to the different areas of the application:

- **Workplace** accesses individual activities and the personal queues and calendar as well as accounts (companies) and contacts.
- **Sales** shows the leads and the full sales cycle including customers, opportunities, quotations, orders, and invoices.
- **Marketing** allows the planning, creation, and monitoring of marketing campaigns and associated campaign response information.
- **Service** allows the creation of service contracts and the monitoring of progress on customer service cases.
- **Settings** allows access to the customisation features of CRM.
- **Resources** covers links to the CRM internet community moderated by Microsoft.

Selecting the **workplace-contacts** area provides an example of a **view** of a CRM entity. The selected view shows the appropriate list of contacts (in this case active contacts owned by the currently logged on user).

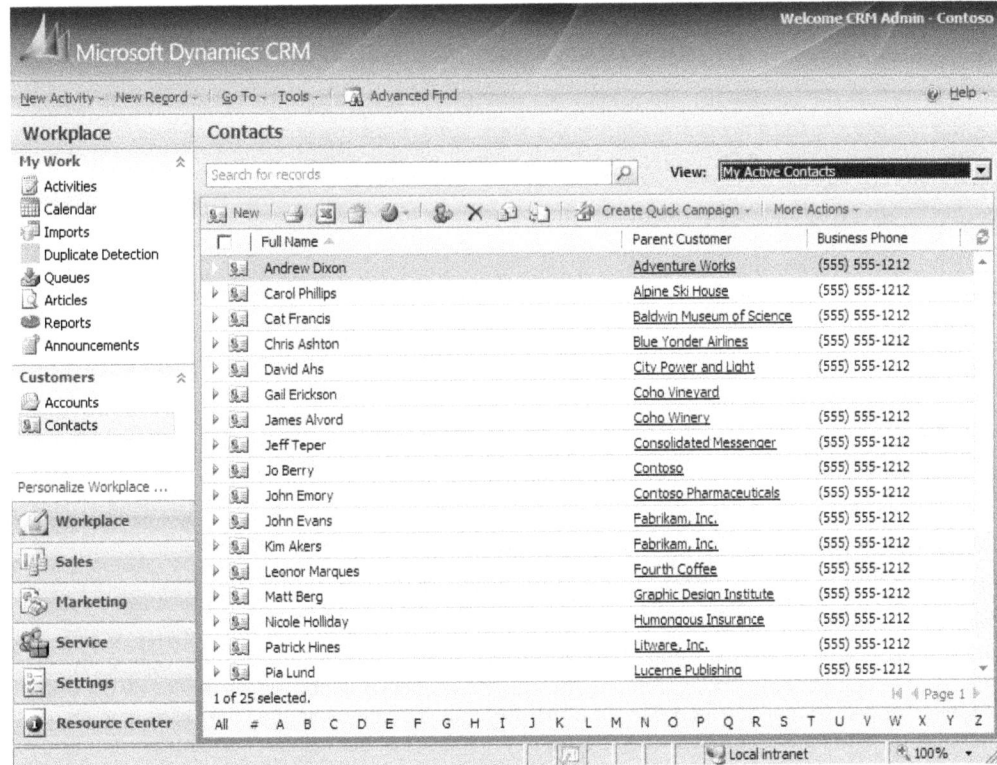

We use this chapter to introduce many of the usability aspects of CRM:

- The **application toolbar** buttons across the top of the page above the title access general functions such as adding new activities and records.
- The **navigation pane** on the left hand side accesses the different work areas available to the user.
- The **view selection** dropdown allows you to filter the records displayed in the list.
- The **view toolbar** controls functionality that applies to the selected records including reports, exporting to excel or word, assigning ownership, and actions specific to the entity.
- The **alphabet bar** and the **page navigation** buttons along the bottom of the view aid navigation.

5.1. Views

Searching for a contact involves selecting the appropriate **view** from the combo box at the top right of the window or searching for a value by typing the search text in the textbox at the top of the list and pressing the adjacent icon.

*Note: The * character can be used as a **wildcard** to allow a search for text contained within a field instead of searching on the start of the field.*

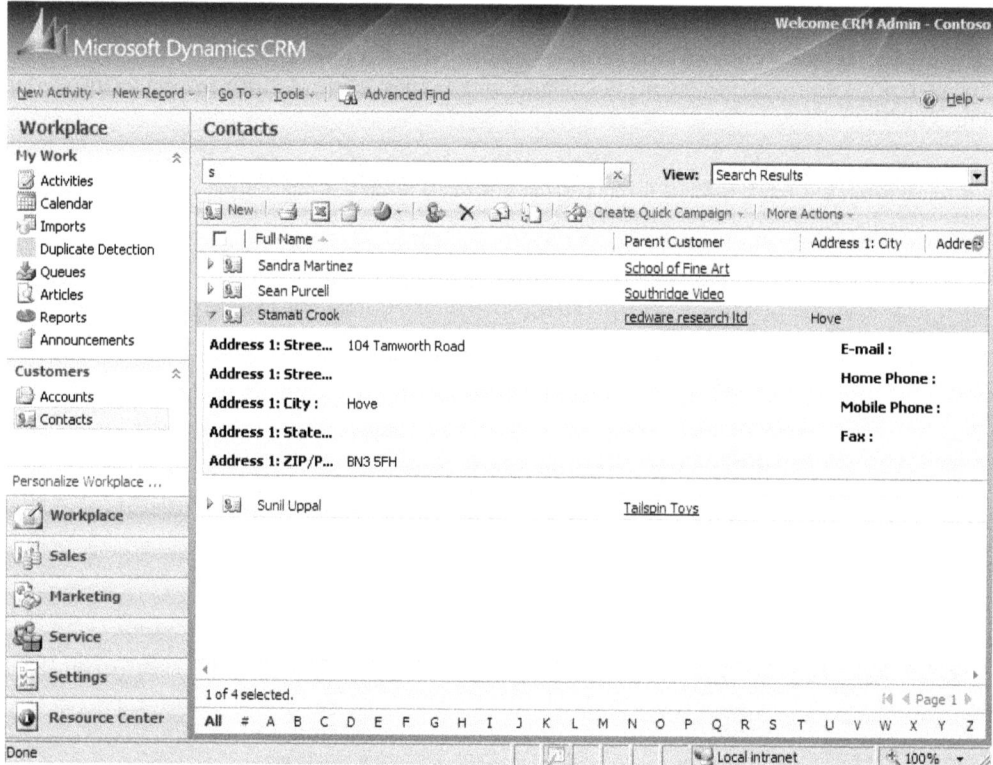

The columns displayed in a view can be **sorted** by clicking on the arrow just to the right of the field name and the column **resized** by dragging the column divider. Select a single record by clicking on the item or individual multiple records with **control+click**. You can select all the records in the current list by clicking the **select all checkbox** at the top left of the column headings.

Just above the column headings is the **view toolbar** which accesses functions that may be applied to the currently selected records in the view. These include:

- **New**. Create a new entity occurrence.
- **Print**. Print a default listing.
- **Export to Excel**. Export to a standalone Excel spreadsheet or dynamic pivot table or spreadsheet (dynamic spreadsheets will update with the latest data). This option also allows data to be exported and modified and the changes re-imported.
- **Mail Merge**. Mail merge to Word.
- **Reports**. Run the appropriate reports.
- **Assign**. Assign to another user (you can **share** from the **more actions** menu).
- **Delete**. Delete the currently selected records (you can **deactivate** records from the **more actions** menu instead of deleting).
- **Send Direct Email**. Sends an email from a template directly without requiring you to edit the message.
- **Merge**. Merge allows you to combine two records if one is a duplicate of the other. The master record inherits all of the activities of the subordinate record which is deactivated.
- **Create Quick Campaign**. Create activities quickly for the selected records (available only on accounts, leads and companies).
- **Run Workflow**. Runs workflow rules to perform required actions (this appears only if there is workflow defined against the entity).
- **More Actions**. See below.

The **More Actions** button accesses general functions that can be applied to the currently selected records in the view. The functions include:

- **Edit**. Brings up a blank form to allow you to set values on all the selected records (the option for editing multiple records might be denied depending on your security settings).
- **Sharing**. Share the record with other users or members of a **team**.
- **Activate**. Records can be activated and deactivated rather than deleted.
- **Deactivate**. Use this instead of delete to keep a history.
- **Detect Duplicates**. See the data management section.
- **Copy Shortcut**. Copies a URL of the current form to the clipboard (you can also use **control+n** to reveal the URL in the browser).
- **Send Shortcut**. Email the URL of the current form to a colleague.
- **Add to Marketing List**. Add record(s) to a marketing list (only for selected entities).
- **Add Relationship**. Define a relationship with another record for contacts, accounts, and opportunities.

The **see more triangle** at the left of each record can be toggled to view more information before selecting the record, and the letters at the bottom of the window provide an **alphabet bar** to select records in accordance with the sort column. Note also the **page navigation** button at the bottom right of the window.

Double clicking on the record in the view listing will open a new window containing the appropriate **form** for the record which allows changes to be made to the data and additional functionality to be accessed. **Related entities** are represented on a view as a column containing the primary attribute of the related entity as a hyperlink. Clicking on this **navigation link** will open the form for the related entity rather than the view entity (causing some confusion to novice users).

5.2. Forms

Each entity has a single **form** which pops up in a standalone web page (you need to disable the popup blocker in your browser). A **navigation pane** on the left hand side of each form allows access to related entities.

The fields containing data for the relevant entity are shown with a series of **tabs** across the top to allow additional areas of the form to be viewed (the arrangement of fields over these tabs is easily customised).

The **Notes** tab is interesting as this allows date-stamped notes to be recorded and **documents** to be loaded against the entity by pressing the **paperclip** icon in the form toolbar.

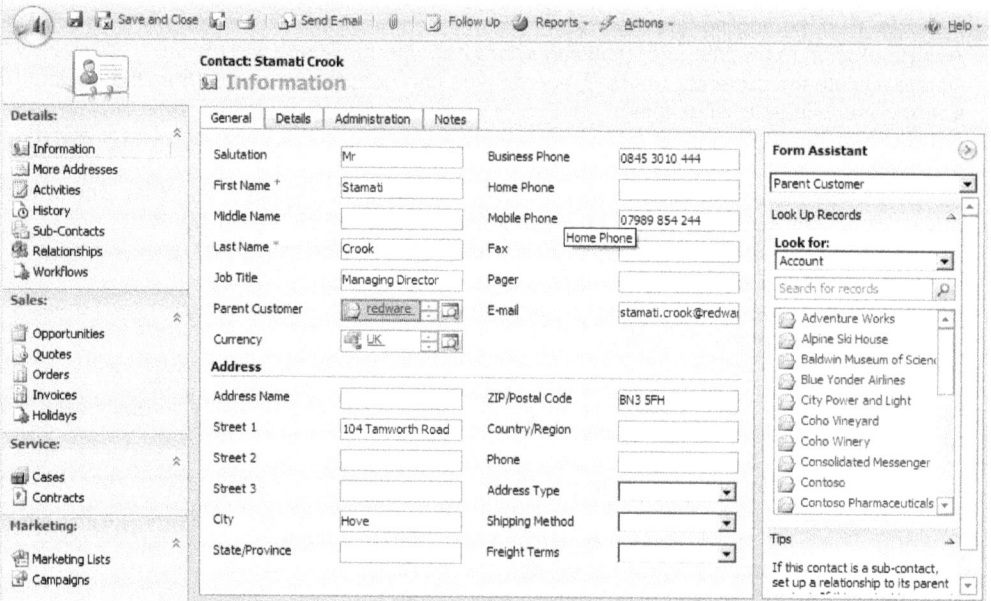

The form has a selection of buttons along the top to save and close the window along with additional buttons which may be specific to the entity or your CRM installation. Pay attention to the **Actions** button which accesses functionality specific to the entity.

Some of the more common buttons in the form toolbar include:

- **Save** to save the current record but keep the window open so that you can then select one of the related entities.
- **Save and Close**.
- **Save and New** to save the current record and create a new blank record.
- **Delete**.
- **Follow Up** to quickly create a related activity using the form assistant.
- **Send Email**. Brings up an email form to create and send a custom email.
- **Reports**.
- **Attach a File**. The paper clip is used to attach a file into the notes section of the form.
- **Run Workflow**. See the workflow section.
- **Assign** to change the owner of the record to another user (or queue) or assign it to yourself.
- **Actions** to add a new activity or perform workflow or access functionality specific to the entity.

You can easily change data by overwriting the current value in the field remembering to press the **save** button after you have finished editing the record. Sometimes a record is **read-only** and you can view but cannot edit it as the fields are all greyed out (security is determined by the owner of the record).

Notice the **lookup window** that appears when clicking on the lookup button to the right of a field for a related entity. CRM also has **auto-response** which is an intelligent way of entering data into fields which require you to select a record from a related entity. You can simply enter the required text directly in the field and **tab** out of the field leaving CRM to search for the best match for you.

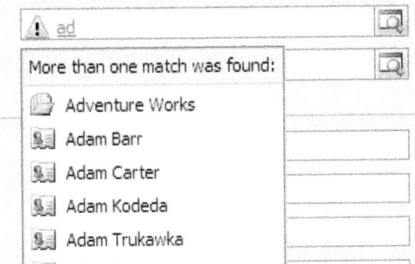

Use semi-colons in the auto-response field to select multiple values where appropriate. You will see an exclamation mark if there is more than one possible value and you can then click on the exclamation mark (or the lookup button) to see a list for a partial search based upon the characters already typed.

Note the **Form Assistant** button to the right of the data entry area which you can expand to show a helper area. The available options are shown in a combo box at the top of the form assistant and are selected as you enter the corresponding field in the data entry area. The form assistant displays a lookup of the appropriate records so you can make a quick selection without popping up the lookup window.

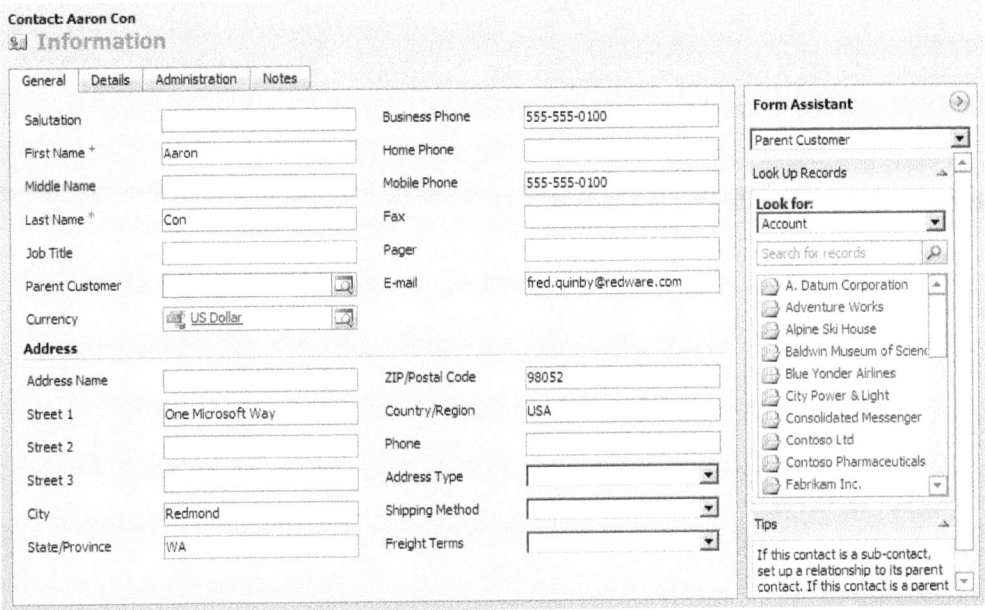

5.3. Notes and Attachments

Most entities have a **notes and attachments** area which allows a time-stamped comment to be entered by a user:

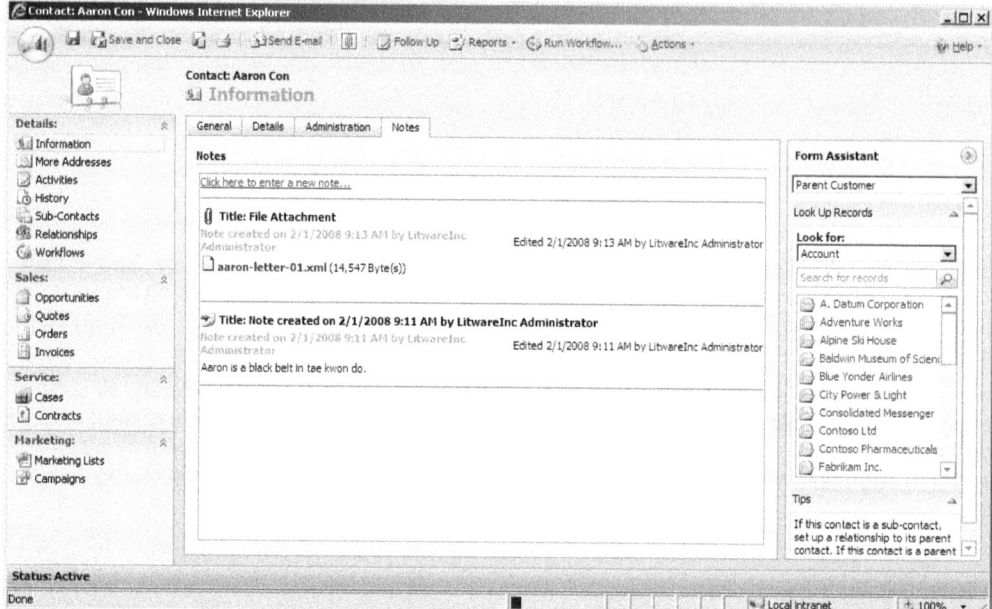

Attachments are added with the **paperclip** (or from the actions menu) and prompt for you to attach the file by selecting a file from your local hard drives. The document is stored in the CRM database and is made available to all users.

5.4. Advanced Find

The **Advanced Find** option on the View page can be used to configure selection criteria to filter data as required. The following screenshot shows how to set up a View on Accounts for **relationship type** customers only.

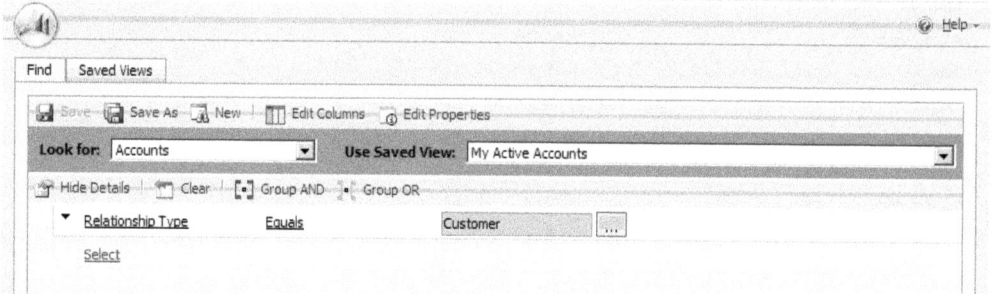

Selection criteria can bring in fields from related entities. The following example filters Contacts for prospects or customers with incomplete Task activities. In this example, the (many-to-one) relationship to the **primary account** is used to check the relationship category, and the (one-to-many) relationship to **Tasks** is used to check for the presence of incomplete tasks.

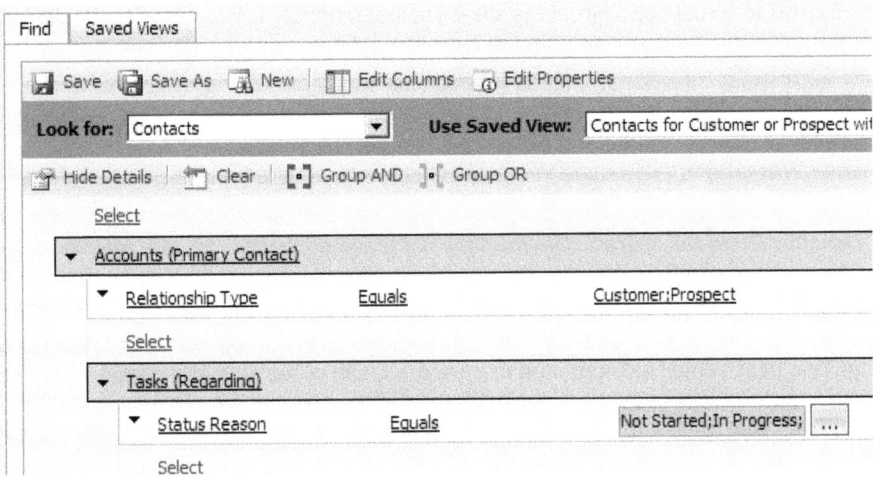

You can **save a view** and it will appear in the drop down list for the appropriate entity (you may need to refresh your browser) and you can also select the saved view and **share** it with other users or teams. The system customiser can create views for all to see using a very similar interface.

You can also **edit the columns** shown in a view and change the width and order of the columns as well as selecting which column is the default sort order. Designing a view with the required fields in combination with the export to Excel functionality provides a handy way for performing regular reporting or data export procedures.

You can select fields from related entities in a View (they must be in a many to one relationship so there is a maximum of one corresponding record in the related table). You can select any field but you are limited to the primary attribute if you want two degrees of separation to relate records from an entity related to the related entity.

5.5. Exporting CRM data to Excel

All Views can easily export data to Excel (subject to the security settings) and a custom view can be created to contain any fields from related (many-to-one) entities.

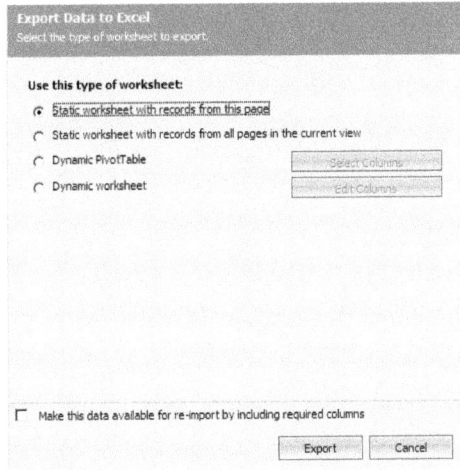

Select the **Export to Excel** button from the View Toolbar (control-click to make a selection of records if required) and then choose from the following options:

- **Static Worksheet**. Simply exports the current view to Excel.
- **Dynamic Pivot Table**. Allows you to make a selection of columns (so you do not have to create a view with all required fields) and export to a dynamic pivot table.
- **Dynamic Worksheet**. Allows you to select the columns required and export to a dynamic Excel file.

Note: Dynamic Excel files extract data from the database each time they are refreshed. The CRM database will use the Windows security of the currently logged on user so that the data returned may be different for each user.

A very useful feature here is the ability to tick the checkbox to **Make the data available for re-importing**. This adds some fields required to track the origin of the data and allows you to email the spreadsheet to a colleague or external contact for updating. You can then re-import the data using the **tools-import data** option, whereupon the changed fields will be updated and new records inserted.

Note: This is perhaps the single most important feature to allow non-programmers to integrate CRM with external systems. It works with custom entities and allows you to both modify and add records.

5.6.   Mail Merge to Word

The view toolbar has a **mail merge** button available on some entities to help create a quick mail merge file to control Microsoft Word (2003 or 2007). Select the required fields by selecting the appropriate view and selecting all records or using **control+click** before pressing the mail merge button.

The mail merge wizard appears and you may specify a **letter**, **fax**, **email** or **label** merge type and optionally choose an existing Word template document stored in CRM.

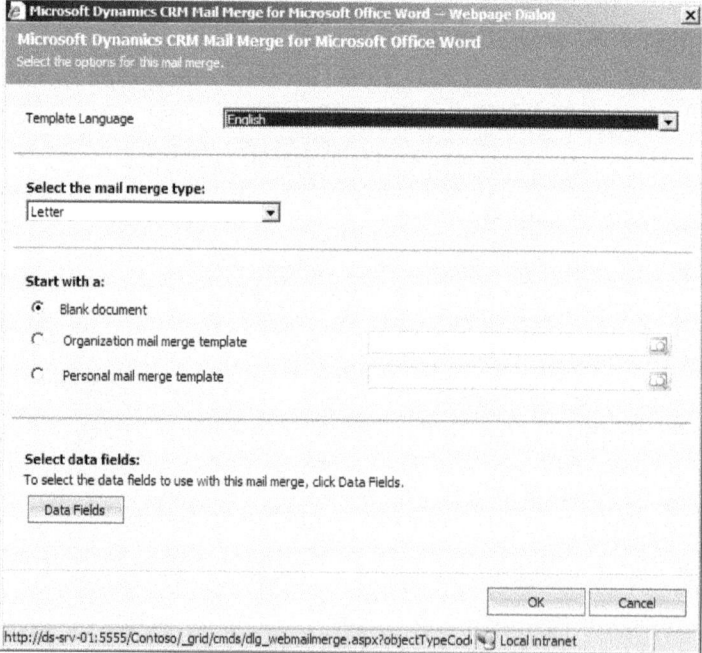

CRM defaults the list of fields exported to Word but allows you to select the fields you require from the appropriate entity together with access to related (many-to-one) entities if required.

The mail merge process will open a Word document on your machine, and you may need to select the **Add Ins** menu at the top of the window and click on the **CRM Mail Merge** macro and **enable macros** on your copy of Word when prompted.

You can perform the mail merge as usual within Word by adding the **address block** and **greeting block** and creating the merged Word document. Word also allows you to create envelopes, labels, directory type listings and email messages in addition to letter mail merge.

Note: *If you use this option from the Outlook Client you will also be prompted if you would like to create the corresponding activity records in CRM (although the letter will not be attached).*

An alternative to mail merge is to use the **export to Excel** option and add the appropriate fields to create a mail merge file that could be used with any word processing package (or sent to an external fulfilment house).

5.7.   Word Templates

Word Templates are added to the system from the **settings-templates-mail merge templates** form and can be uploaded from your hard drive.

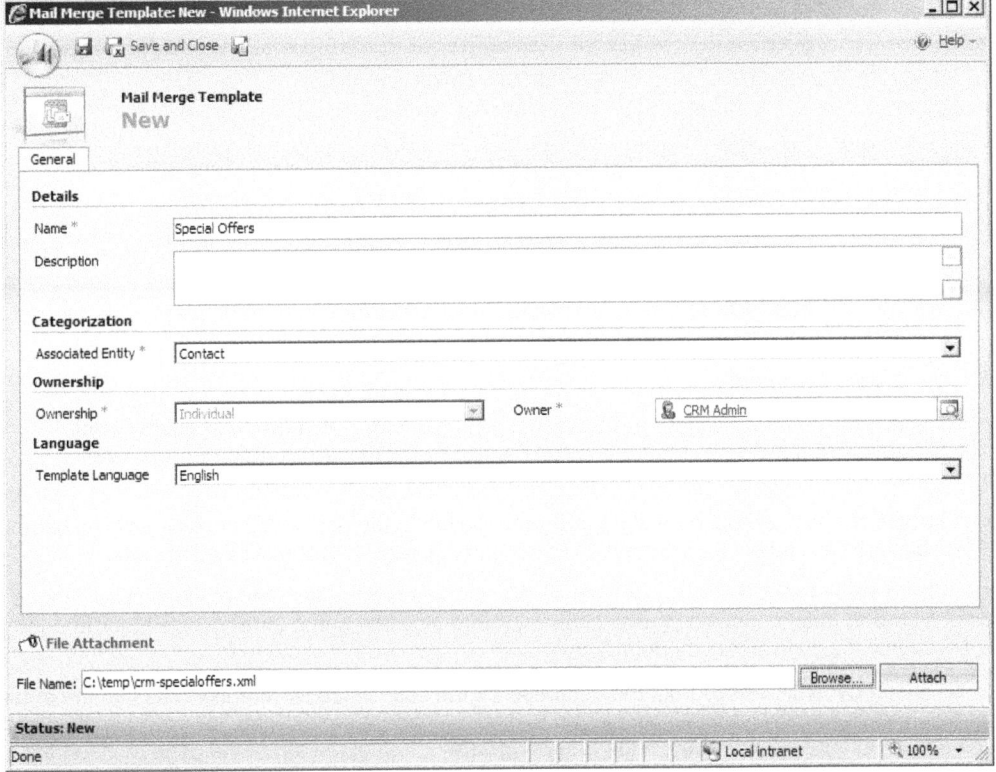

5.8.   Email

The lead, contact and account forms have a **Send Email** button on the toolbar which creates a new email activity. Emails can also be created in a similar manner to other activities using the **new activity** button on the CRM toolbar.

Emails are sent out from the CRM web interface using either SMTP or Exchange (the former are not automatically copied into the Outlook folders). Emails can be typed with simple formatting or created from an **email template** or **knowledge base article** (described in the Services chapter).

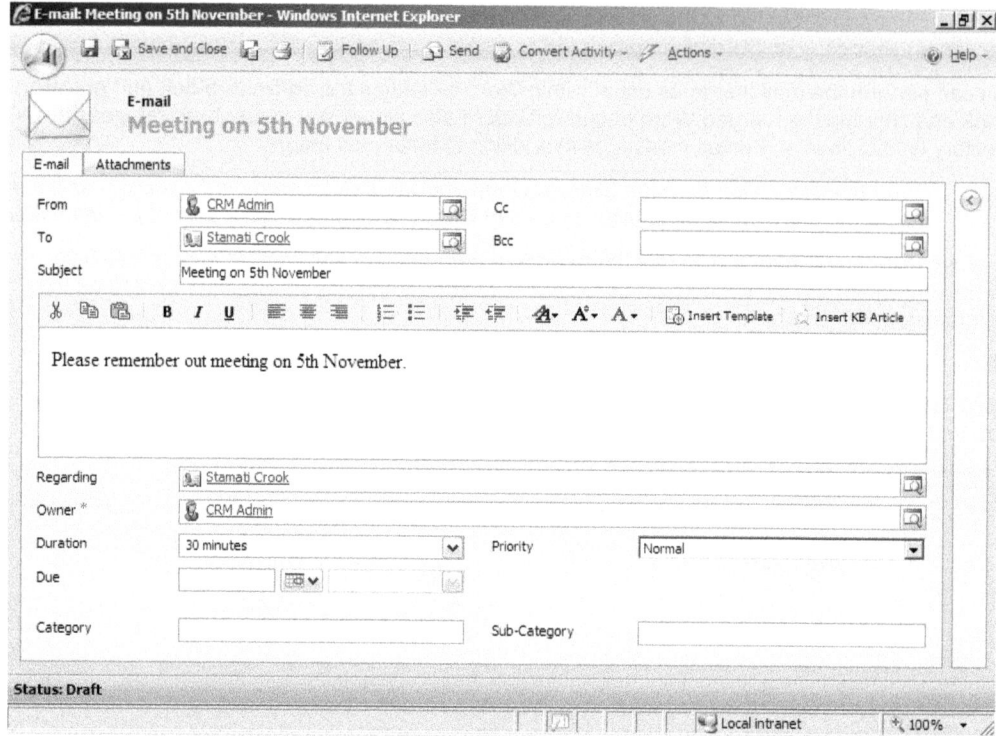

Note: When entering text into an email message, use **enter** for a paragraph line space but use **shift+enter** if you want a line break only with no space.

5.9. Email Templates

Email Templates can be configured system-wide or by each user as a quick productivity aid. Personal Email Templates are created from **tools-options** or the **workplace-personalize workspace** option in CRM or the **CRM-options** menu in the Outlook client.

You may type text with simple formatting using the toolbar in the edit space or open an html page in Internet Explorer and select the contents to paste into the page for sophisticated layouts.

Be careful to design your HTML to use images that are available at an internet location as images are not stored or transmitted along with the email. Note also that some email clients block images and show only the plain HTML by default.

You can insert dynamic values from the database for the associated CRM entity data into the email. User field values are always available for you to design a signature showing, for example, the user name and telephone number. Select the **Insert/Update** button at the top of the page to insert the required data field with an optional value to show if the data field is blank. The entities available will depend on the base entity selected when you create the template.

Note: It does not seem possible to define attachments for a template which need to be added each time (or created using workflow).

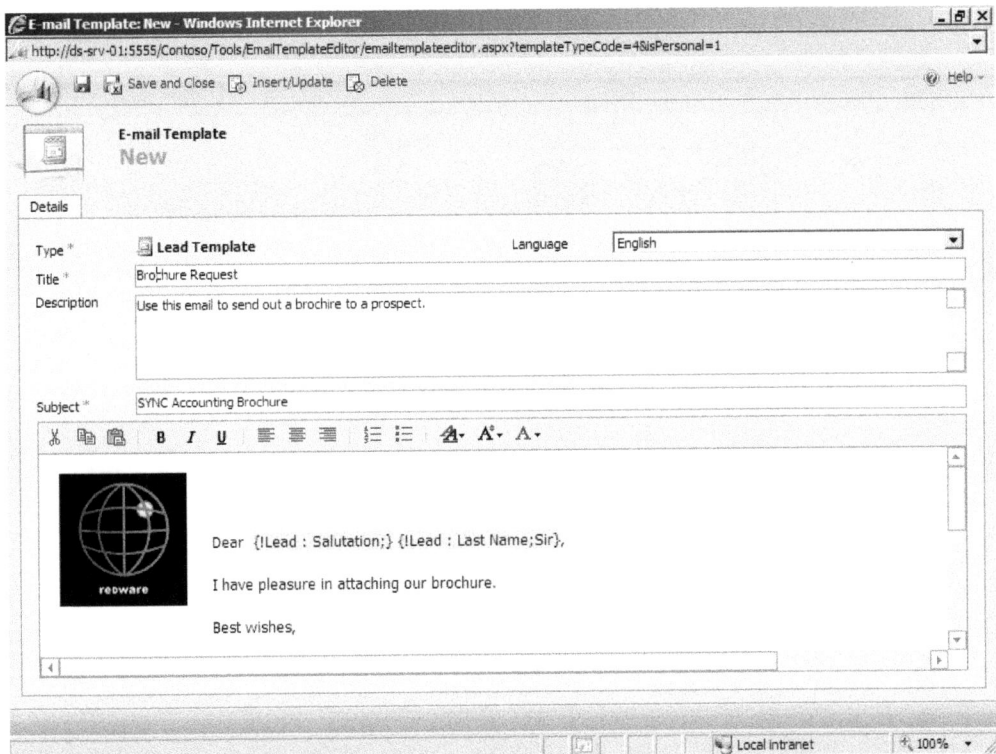

Specifying style information is difficult via the user interface because it is not possible to edit the html header information to define a style or add a style sheet. Consequently you must control the style information by using the formatting buttons or with inline styles.

The easy way to create sophisticated email templates is to create the web page with inline styles and save and open the file in Internet Explorer for pasting into the template. The inline styles will be preserved when you paste and the underlying HTML for an inline style looks like this:

```
<p style="font-family: Arial, Helvetica, sans-serif; font-size: 12px">Thank you for
taking the time to talk with me about our software add-ons for Microsoft CRM 3.0.
We currently offer the following functionality: </p>
```

5.10. Send Direct Email

The **Send Direct E-mail** button is available on the toolbar of some views and allows you to send a template email straight off to one or more contacts without needing to view or edit the emails. Select the required view and **control+click** to select the required records and then press the **Send Direct E-mails** button, select the email template, and the emails are sent and automatically stored in the activity history.

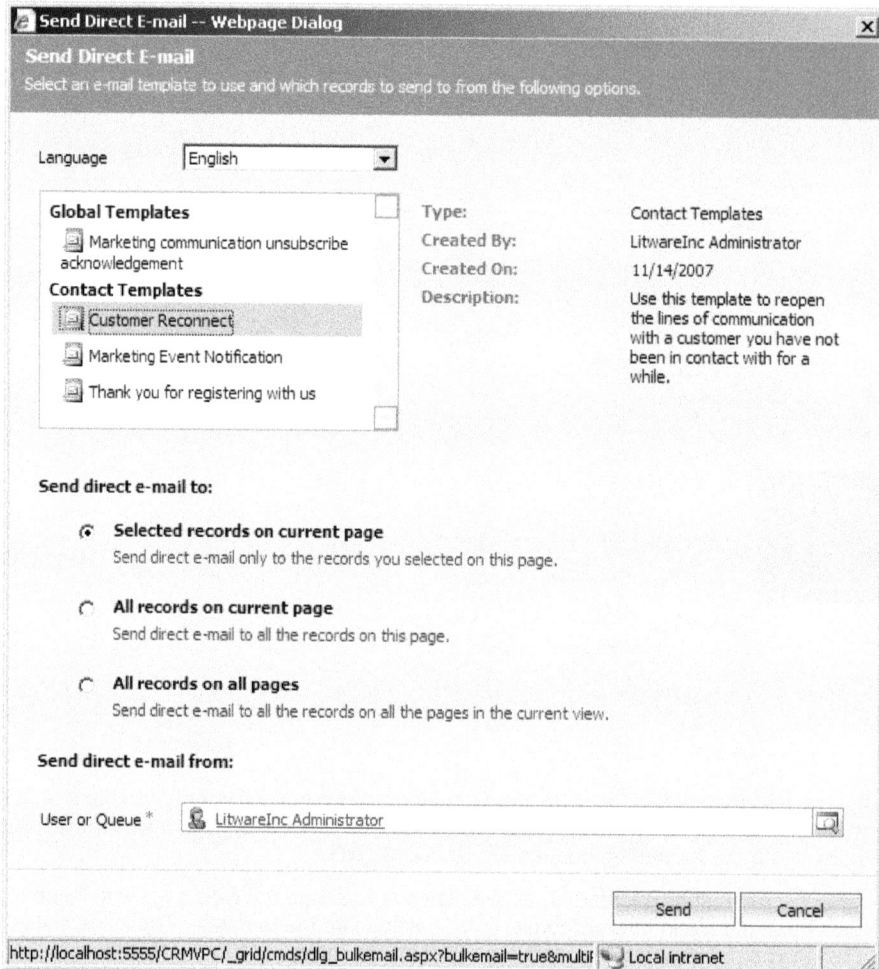

5.11. Quick Campaigns

The **Quick Campaign** button on the view toolbar allows activities to be created for each record selected. This might be useful to schedule outbound phone calls or to create emails or activities quickly without using a marketing list or proper campaign (see the Marketing section for more details).

Selecting the Quick Campaign button prompts you to choose an activity type and then displays a template form for you to set the values required into the generated activities. You can use dynamic field values to enter details from the corresponding records.

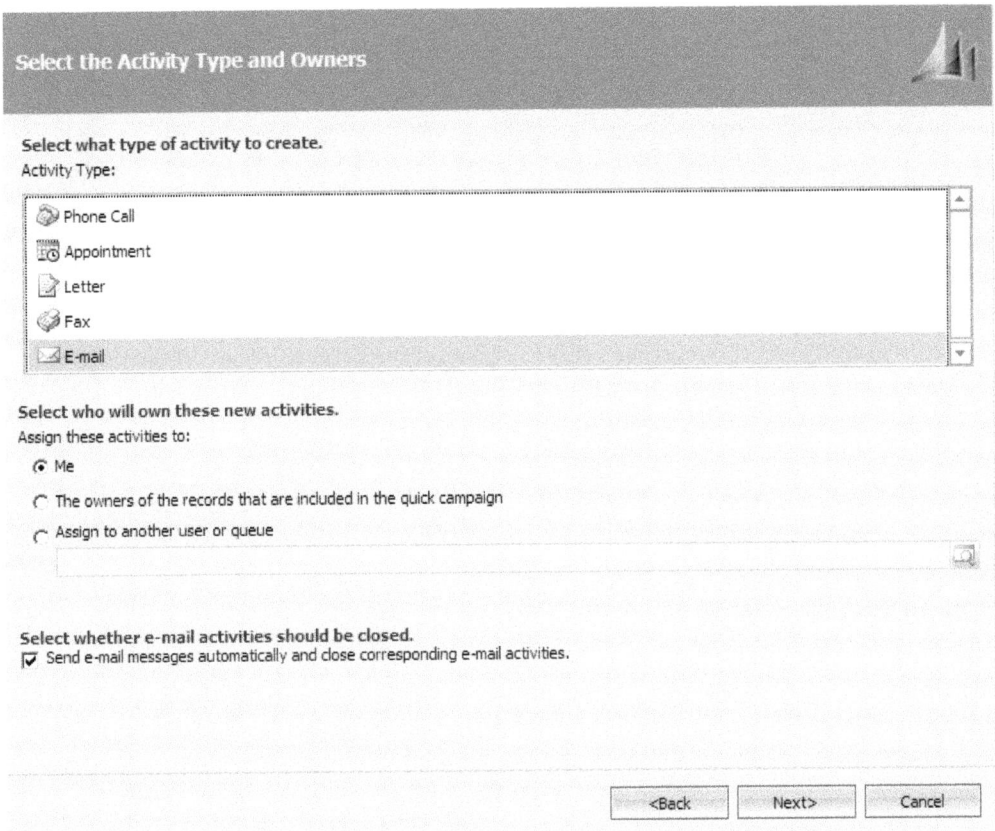

Note: The checkbox at the bottom of the quick campaign allows you to send out the generated emails immediately.

5.12. Sharing and Assignment

Security is set up according to the owner of each record (see the chapter on security). Each owner belongs to a business unit which determines the security settings and whether other users can read the data and write and perform other activities on the record.

CRM allows you to change the current owner of the entity occurrence using the assignment option from the **actions-assign** option which is available on the toolbar for most entities (if you have permissions). Changing the owner will change the security settings and you may no longer be able to view or edit the data in certain situations.

Note: Assigning is the same as changing the value of the owner field.

Sharing the entity occurrence with the **actions-sharing** option does not change or overwrite the security setting but allows other users or teams access to the entity occurrence.

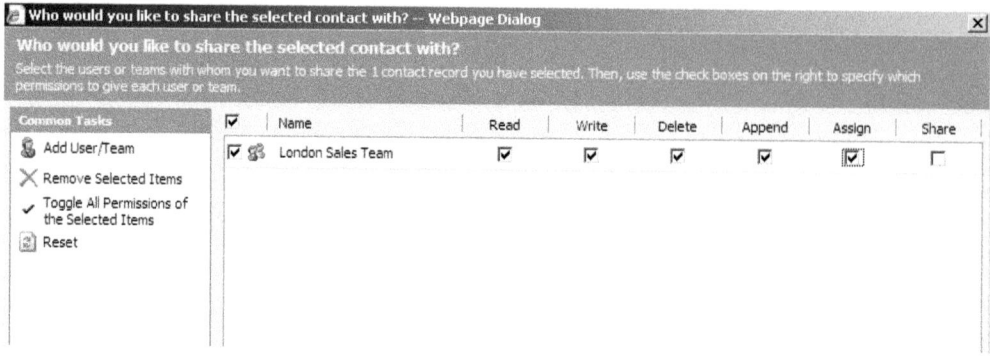

6. Customers

One important point to note about Accounts and Contacts is that both can be considered as **Customers** for the purposes of the sales cycle. Opportunities, quotations, orders and invoices can be specified against either Accounts or Contacts as required (there does not seem to be a way to configure just B2B or B2C commerce).

6.1. Accounts

Accounts in CRM refer to companies and not just sales accounts. Many installations rename this entity to avoid confusion.

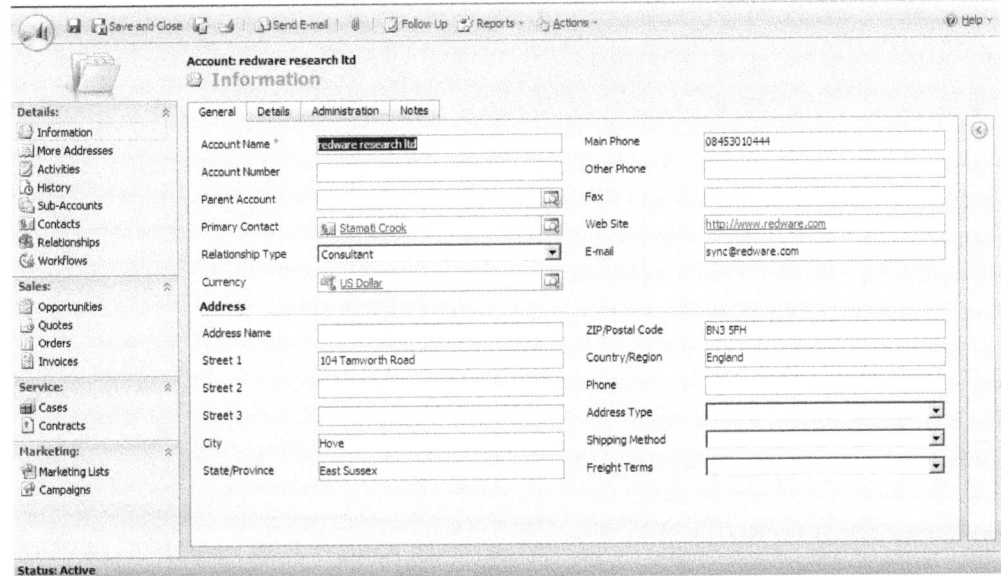

Some notes about Accounts:

- The **primary contact** can be used to specify the default contact.
- Select the contacts view from the left hand pane and add a new contact to copy the address and other fields across to the new contact automatically (in accordance with the mappings set up in the customisation).
- The **relationship type** is a convenient field to categorise companies as suppliers, competitors, customers, prospects and so forth.
- Accounts have a **currency** which is automatically applied to new contacts when they are added from the contacts pane.
- Two addresses can be stored in the entity, with additional addresses stored by selecting the **addresses** view on the left hand pane.
- The **parent customer** can be used to specify the ownership hierarchy of groups and companies.

6.2. Contacts

Contacts contain the standard contact information and the **parent customer** usually specifies the company for which the contact works.

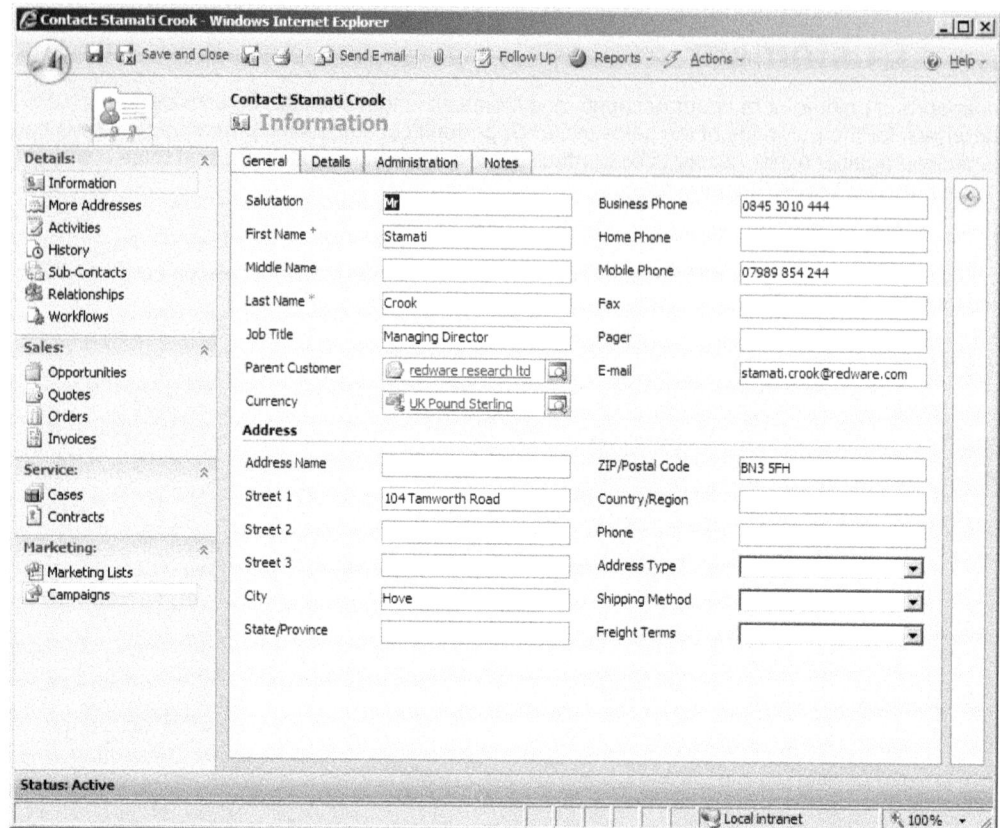

Note: One feature of CRM is that the Company details for a contact must be specified separately in the associated account record even if there is only one contact recorded against the company

6.3. Relationship Roles

See the customisation section.

7. Activities

Activities are used to schedule or record events and are each assigned an **owner** who is responsible for completing the activity in accordance with the best practices of your organisation. The following types of activity are available:

- **Task**.
- **Fax**.
- **Email**.
- **Letter**.
- **Phone Call**.
- **Appointment**.
- **Service Activity** (see the service chapter).
- **Campaign Response** (see the marketing chapter).

Most of the core entities and custom entities that allow user ownership have activities and notes attached to them. New activities can be created for an entity in several ways:

- From the **new-activity** option in the CRM Toolbar.
- From the **action-add activity** menu in the Form menu.
- Selecting New when looking at the **activities pane** for the entity.
- Using the **follow up** button from the form toolbar.
- Using the follow up option in the **form assistant**.
- Selecting the **workplace-activities** pane and adding a new activity.

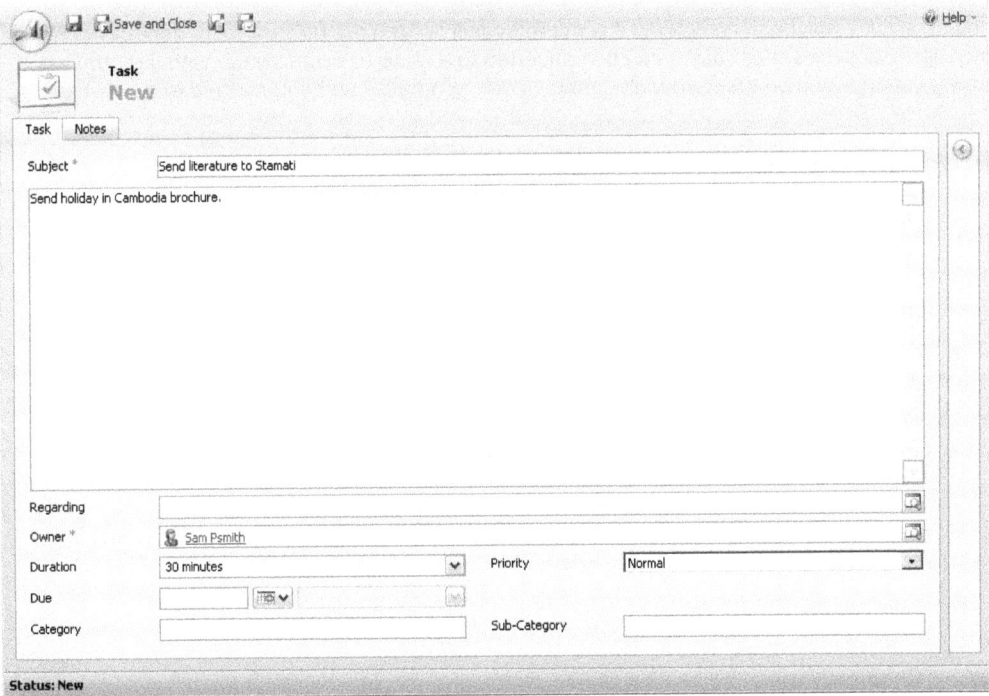

Activities can also be created automatically using workflow when a new opportunity is created for example. Incoming email activities can be created automatically when sent to an email address defined in a queue or when received in response to an email sent out from CRM. Activities can also be created from the Outlook Client for CRM by pressing the **Track in CRM** button.

Activities can be viewed from the **workplace-activities** view or from the **activities** pane against each Entity. Each activity is owned by a user (or a queue) who will undertake responsibility for completion of the task.

Note: Take care when creating custom entities as only user-owned entities can have associated activities.

The following fields are present on all activities:

- **Owner**.
- **Subject**. A short one-line description.
- **Description**.
- **Regarding**. The entity record to which the activity relates could be any core CRM entity or user-owned custom entity.
- **Scheduled Start** (the due field).
- **Duration**.
- **Priority**.
- **Category** and **Sub-Category** for your own text categorisations.

The following fields are also maintained in addition to those on the default form:

- **Actual Start** (automatically filled in on completion).
- **State**. The state of the activity entity, usually open or completed.
- **Status**. A breakdown status relating to each state.

Once an activity has been completed it is made available from the **history** pane against each related entity. Many activities (not Tasks) can be converted to a **case** or **opportunity** with the **convert activity** button found on the form toolbar and incoming emails can be converted to a new **lead**.

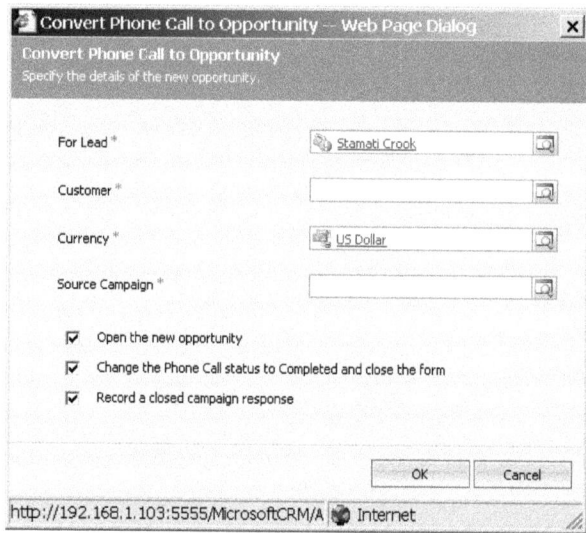

Note: **Read-only** users will be able to view their activities but not update them.

32   Microsoft CRM 4.0 User Handbook

7.1. Tasks

Tasks are the catch-all activity type used to schedule and manage workflow activities and are synchronised with Exchange into the **Task List** within Outlook.

7.2. Email

Outgoing email activities can be created manually or from an email template (see the Using CRM section) and replies tracked and stored against the correct entity if you have set up the Email Router for CRM or the synchronisation options for the Outlook Client correctly.

Standard emails can be defined with a template and dispatched with the **send direct email button** or with a quick campaign.

7.3. Fax

The fax activity does not appear to be integrated with the Microsoft fax solutions. Ideally the incoming fax should recognise the telephone number and create a fax activity (with the attached fax document) against the appropriate lead, contact or account. This currently needs to be done manually or programmatically.

7.4. Phone Call

Phone call records are used for scheduling **outbound** phone calls and recording notes for **inbound** calls. Some third party telephony applications automatically create phone call records for inbound calls.

Phone calls and faxes have additional activity fields:

- The direction of the call (incoming or outgoing).
- The sender or recipient.
- Phone or Fax number.
- Fax Cover.

Note: *TAPI dialling is possible with the Outlook client but not currently with the web interface for CRM, and incoming call solutions are available from a limited number of telephony vendors (including Cisco and Avaya). The author has a solution for telephony at http://www.redware.com/mscrm.*

7.5. Letter

Letter activities can be created manually or as part of the mail merge process when using the Outlook client for mail merge to Word.

Documents are not automatically attached and you may like to use mail merge on a single record to create a document and then add the letter activity and attach the document into the notes area using the paperclip on the toolbar.

7.6. Appointment

Appointments are more complex activities that allow several **resources** to be booked. The example below shows a meeting booked for a contact and a user with an optional extra user attending. The resources that can be booked for an appointment comprise:

- **User**.
- **Lead**, **Contact** or **Account**.
- **Equipment** and **Resources** (for example, a meeting room or a projector).

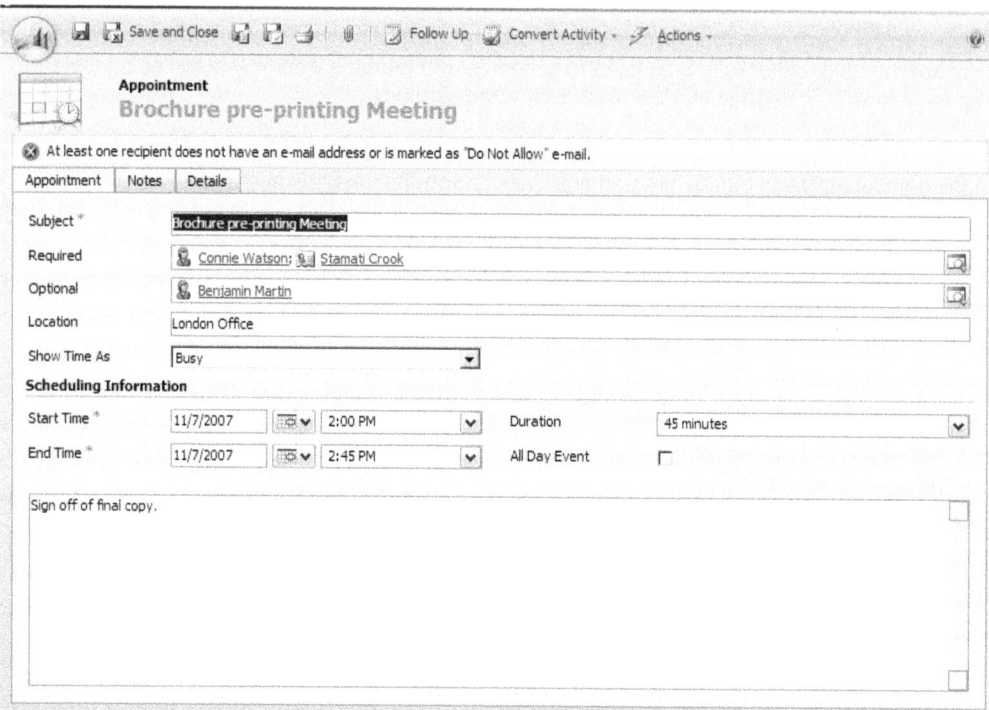

Appointments are recorded in the calendars available from the **workplace-calendar** and the **service-calendar** areas and within the **Exchange Calendar** in Outlook once the activity has been synchronised. Use the **save as completed** option to clear the appointment from the diary after it has taken place.

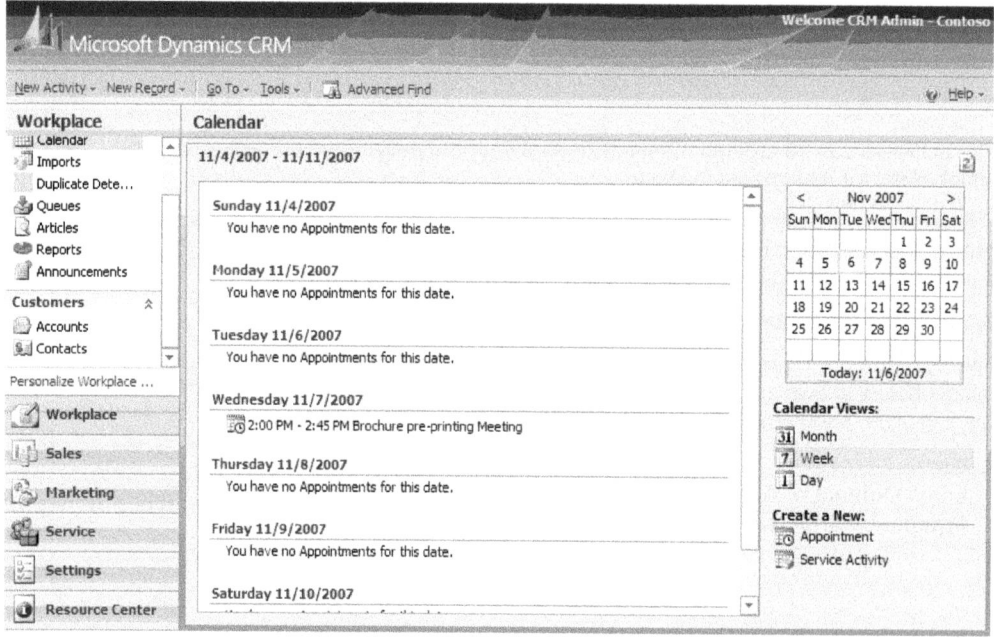

7.7. Service Activity

Service activities are similar to appointments but allow equipment or a package of required resources to be defined and automatically scheduled when available (see the services chapter).

7.8. Campaign Response

Campaign Response activities are used to monitor the success of marketing campaigns (see the marketing chapter).

8. Outlook Client

CRM is available both from a web browser and from the Outlook Client for CRM. The two versions have identical functionality and identical user interfaces.

Remote users who are not able to access CRM with a web browser directly or over a VPN will need to use the Laptop Client for Outlook with local data and synchronise data periodically when they reconnect to the network.

The screenshot below shows the Outlook 2007 client for CRM displaying the contacts view window within the Outlook interface. You can see that the full CRM user interface is made available within Outlook, together with the same arrangement of work areas in the left hand navigation area.

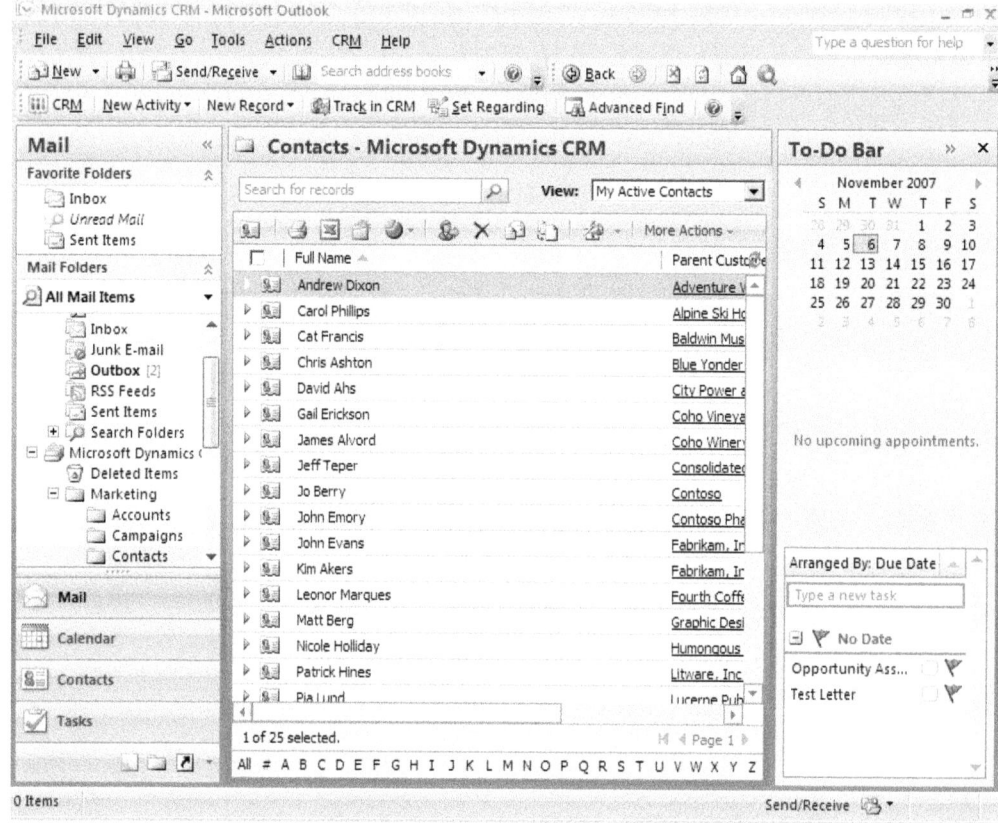

The **CRM menu** within Outlook also accesses the navigation structure and allows new activities or other CRM data to be created. The **CRM Toolbar** also offers these options:

- Create a **new activity**.
- Create a **new record** for a CRM entity.
- **Track in CRM** allows an existing Outlook contact, task, appointment or email to be added to CRM and any changes to the data (in either application) automatically synchronised.
- **Tasks** originating in Outlook can also be tracked and you can choose whether to create a task, letter, phone call, or fax activity.

- **Set Regarding** allows the regarding object for an task or email to be specified quickly within Outlook without having to launch the CRM window (the related entity does not have to be a contact).
- **Set Parent** replaces the Set Regarding button for a contact and sets the parent customer record.
- **Advanced Find** allows you to create your own views in CRM.

The following CRM functions are provided in addition to Outlook functionality:

- Contacts (owned by the user) are copied into the Contacts section to allow contact details from CRM to be used within Outlook. Tracked contacts can have the **parent customer** set with the **Set Parent** button.
- Appointments, tasks, letters, phone calls, emails and contacts originating in CRM can be tracked in Outlook. Data is automatically synchronised and Outlook can be configured to use the CRM forms for these entities (instead of the native Outlook form) to make sure that any custom fields or workflows are available to the user.

Items originating in Outlook are synchronised immediately with CRM as the appropriate track button is pressed. Items originating (and modified) within CRM are synchronised with Outlook at startup and every 15 minutes by default. The **CRM-Synchronise with CRM** menu option can be used to synchronise on demand.

8.1. Tracking Contacts

The Contacts tab in Outlook is modified to show contacts owned by the user in CRM rather than the private Outlook Contacts list (which is still available). Clicking on a contact will bring up an Outlook form containing the contact details synchronised from CRM.

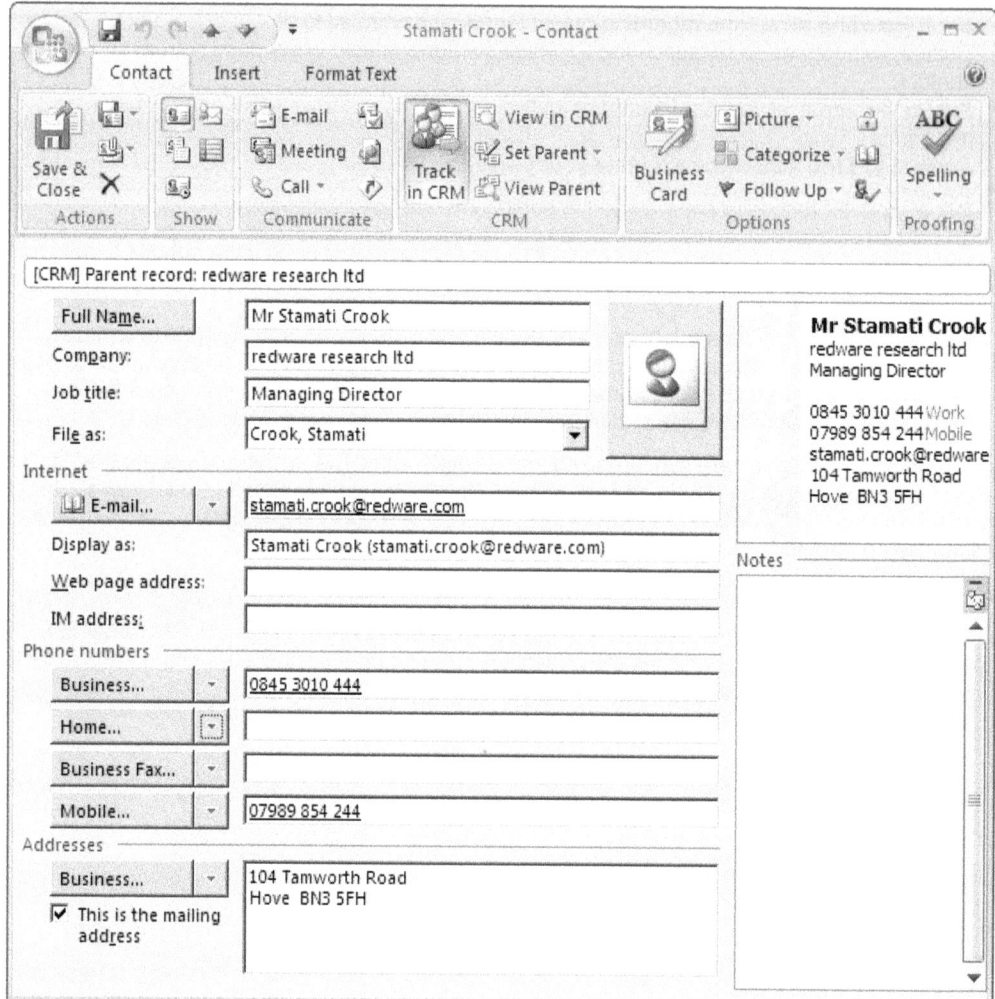

A few of the fields shown on the form are specific to Outlook and are therefore not synchronised with CRM. There will be additional fields specified for the contact entity in CRM that are not shown on the Outlook form.

Some specific CRM functionality is provided in the CRM portion of the toolbar on the contact form:

- Pressing the **View in CRM** button will launch the contact form to allow editing within the CRM interface (and allow access to additional fields and functionality).
- **Set Parent** will show a lookup view to set the parent customer of the contact without having to launch CRM.
- **View Parent** will launch the CRM form for the parent customer.

The main benefit of the Outlook Contact form is the powerful integration that Outlook has with the desktop. The user interface constraints caused by the browser implementation are removed in Outlook and more functionality is available:

- The **Call Contact** option on the actions menu allows outbound calling using **TAPI** to connect to your telephone system or **Instant Messenger**.

- Mail merge is available from the **tools-mail merge** menu when looking at the Outlook (not CRM) view of Contacts in the Outlook client.
- Outlook customisations and third-party add-ons are more numerous than for CRM.
- Macros and other features that apply to a desktop rather than a web application are available.

8.2. Mail Merge in Outlook

The mail merge option from the contacts view within the Outlook Client extends the functionality available from the CRM web application allowing you to create corresponding activities if required.

First select the required contacts with **control+click** and press the **mail merge** button on the view toolbar and perform the mail merge to Word in the usual way.

The **create activities** dialog window appears after finishing the mail merge in Word and allows you to create the corresponding letter activities with the **merged document** automatically attached as a file in the notes field.

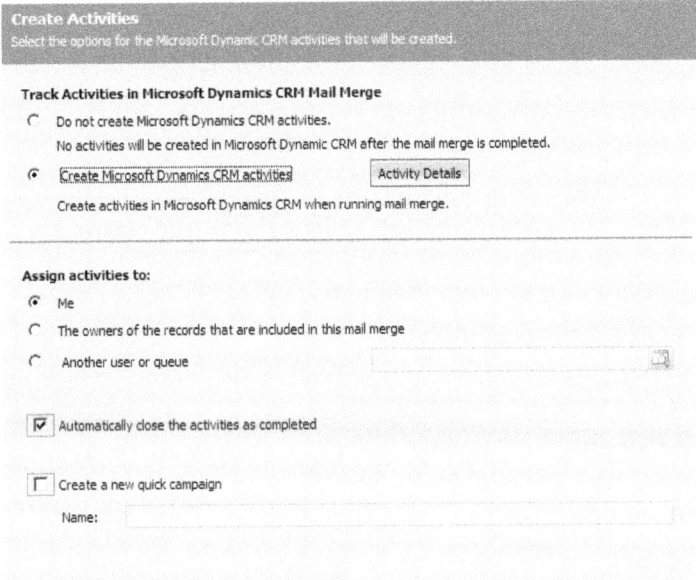

Note: Activities can also be created easily with a Quick Campaign if you are using the web application although the merged document will not be attached in the activity note. See the Using CRM and Marketing chapters for additional mail merge options.

8.3. Tasks

Tasks can easily be synchronised from Outlook to CRM by creating a Task and clicking on the **Track in CRM** button. You have a choice of **task**, **phone call**, **letter**, **fax** and once you have tracked the record you can use the **Set Regarding** button to select the CRM entity occurrence to attach the activity to without having to launch CRM.

Note: Call the synchronisation process from the CRM menu if you need to see new tasks created in CRM immediately.

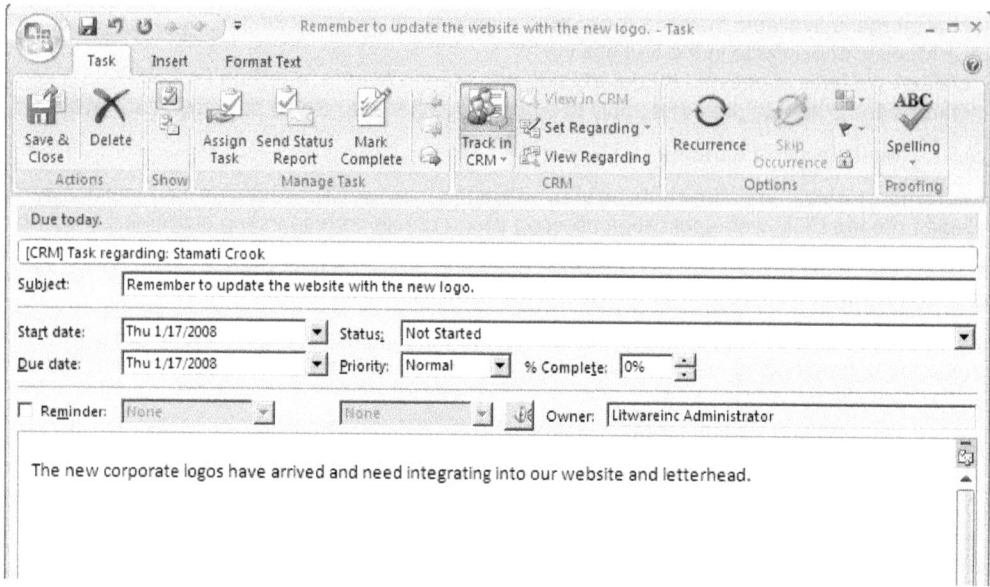

Tasks can easily be completed within Outlook by clicking the **completed** checkbox which will update the corresponding CRM activity and move it to the **History** pane (and remove any reminders).

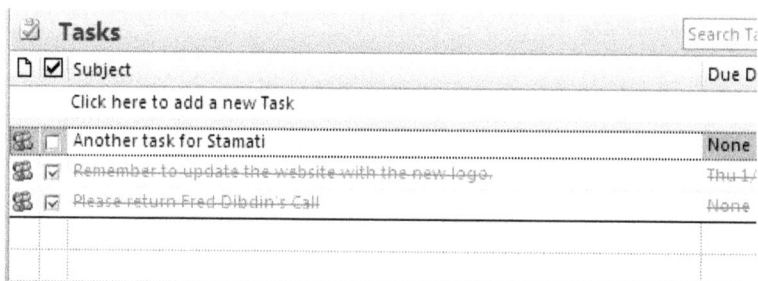

8.4. CRM Options

Outlook and CRM options are set from the CRM menu:

- **General** options allow you to specify whether the Outlook form or the corresponding CRM form is used within Outlook to edit different entities.
- **Synchronization** (see below) controls synchronisation with CRM.
- **Workplace** activates the appropriate work areas in the Outlook navigation pane.
- **Formats** sets regional settings.
- **Email Templates** allows you to maintain CRM email templates.
- **Address Book** specifies how often the address book is updated and can extend the synchronisation of contacts and activities beyond those owned by the current user.
- **Languages** makes use of the language packs.

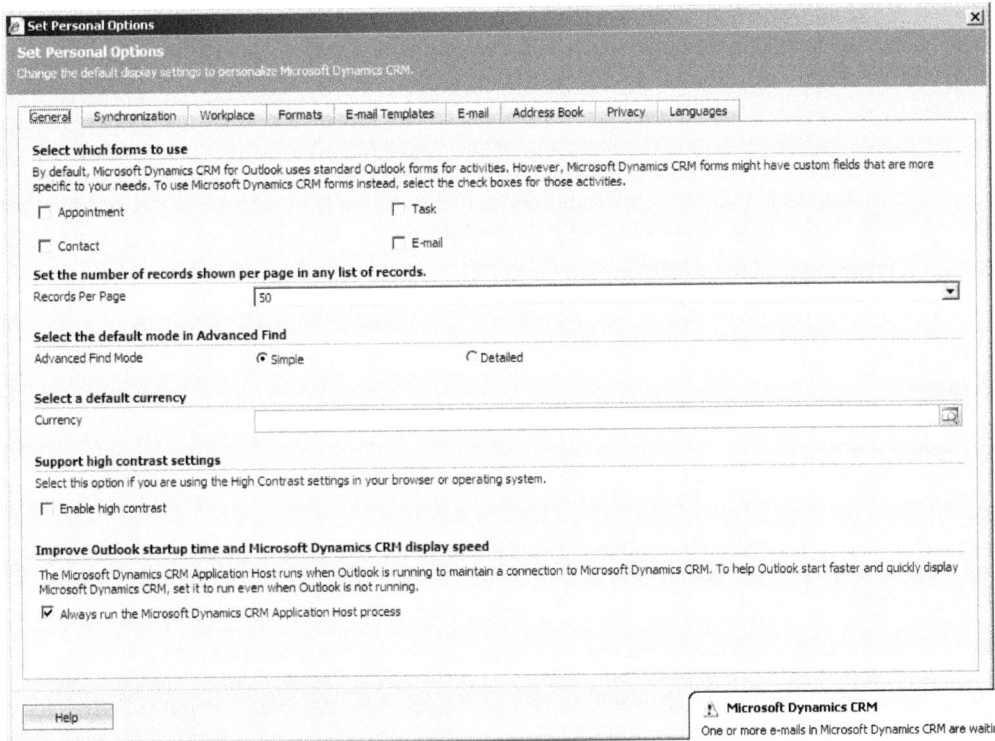

8.5. Email Synchronisation

Emails and email templates can be synchronised with CRM. Email templates are managed either within CRM or from the **CRM-options-email templates** page. Emails have the following synchronisation options:

- Synchronise all emails into CRM.
- Synchronise only emails received that are replies from emails originating in CRM.
- Synchronise only emails that have email addresses belonging to leads, contacts or accounts already entered in CRM (see the **Address Book** options for details).

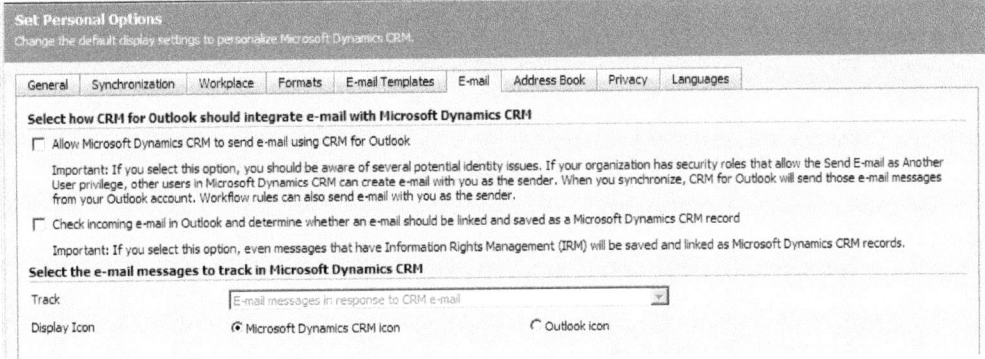

The email router supports both Microsoft Exchange and SMTP/POP3 mail infrastructure but CRM can be configured to ignore the email router and use your local Outlook application to perform all mail synchronisation.

A unique tag can be specified for each outgoing email so that replies are easily matched and stored against the appropriate entity in CRM. Incoming emails with a tag are attached to any customer (contact or account) who matches the email address. The email is also stored against the parent account of the contact if specified. Emails that cannot be matched show the email address as a red hyperlink which allows quick access to create a new contact.

8.6. Tracking and Synchronisation Options

The following items can be synchronised between CRM and Outlook in both directions:

- **Contacts**.
- **Emails**.
- **Tasks**.
- **Appointments**.
- **Phone Calls**.
- **Faxes**.

Pressing the **Track in CRM** button within Outlook immediately creates the associated data within CRM for all to see, whereas data is synchronised into Outlook from CRM at start-up and every 15 minutes by default.

Note: Your appointments and tasks may not be synchronised immediately from CRM with synchronisation taking place only when you run the Outlook application. Note the **CRM Application Host** process which can be configured from the tools-general options if you do not run Outlook often on your desktop.

The **CRM-options-synchronzation** page allows options to be set to clarify which records are downloaded automatically from CRM. This can include appointments, tasks, phone calls, letters, faxes and contacts owned by the user.

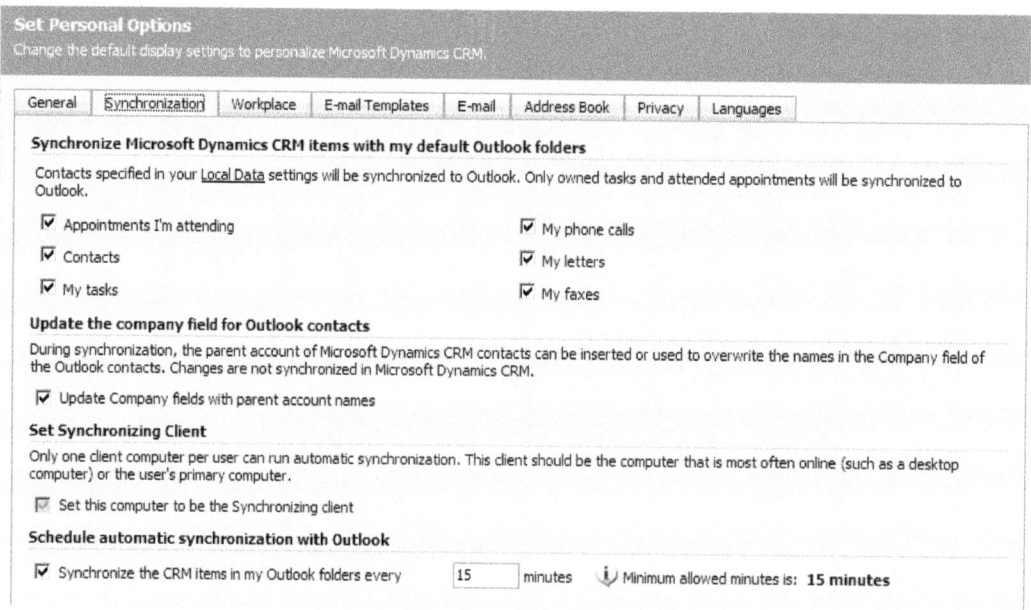

Press the **local data** hyperlink to bring up a view that lets you define a series of advanced find queries to supplement the default synchronisation option which only copy down data that you own. You can use this to add to the contacts copied into your address book for example.

Note: *Synchronisation properties for the company allow the parent company name to be copied down into Outlook for appropriate contacts. Changes to this field are not however synchronised with CRM.*

The **address book** tab allows you to specify how often the address book is updated and which records are downloaded from CRM and defaults to downloading just the records you own. The address book in the Outlook Client automatically creates additional address books to show CRM contacts, leads, users and equipment. Click on the **address book** icon in the Outlook client to search these areas.

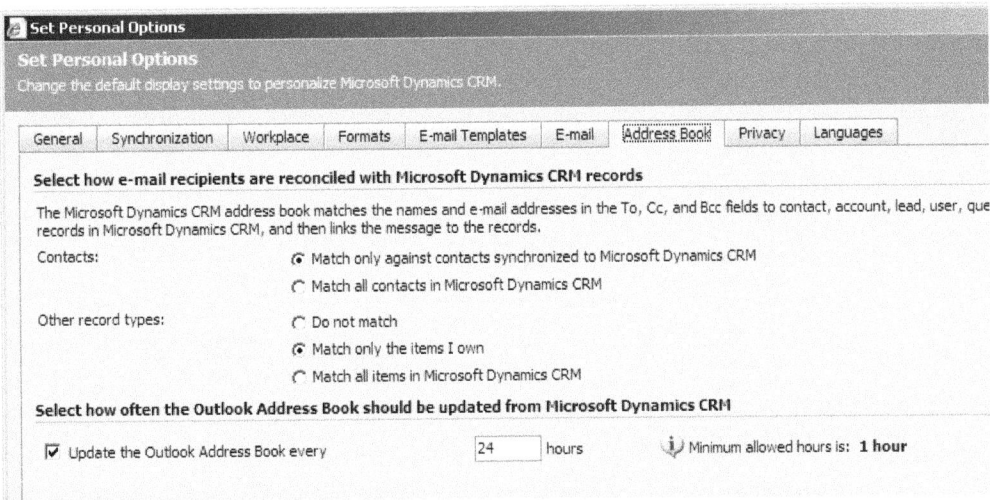

Deleted records may not synchronise between CRM and Outlook as expected. Deleting a completed task in Outlook, for example, does not delete the corresponding CRM record. Deleting a record in CRM may break the link to the Outlook data but not delete the record in Outlook.

8.7.   Laptop Client Synchronisation

The Laptop Client for Outlook stores CRM data locally (up to 4GB) as determined by the filter criteria setup in the **Local Data** option of the CRM menu. Synchronisation can occur in the background and the **Go Offline** option is used before disconnecting the laptop from the network.

Data is synchronised back with CRM when the laptop is reconnected to the system and the process checks to see if the data has been changed by other users since the copy was made. Checks are made on a field by field basis so that different users can change two different fields on the same record without affecting the synchronisation process. See the Microsoft documentation for more details.

8.8.   Diagnostic Tool

A diagnostic tool is provided to help diagnose problems on your machine if the CRM client for Outlook fails to install or operate.

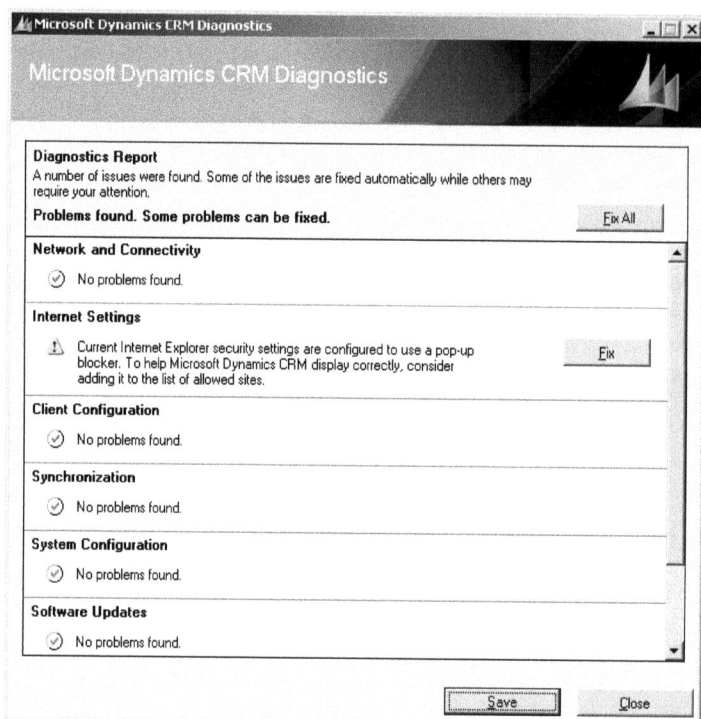

Note: The **fix** button is particularly helpful for novice users who need to remove the popup blocking on their browsers.

9. Workplace

The workplace is often used as the default view for CRM users as it provides easy access to the activities view which allows activities to be filtered in various different ways.

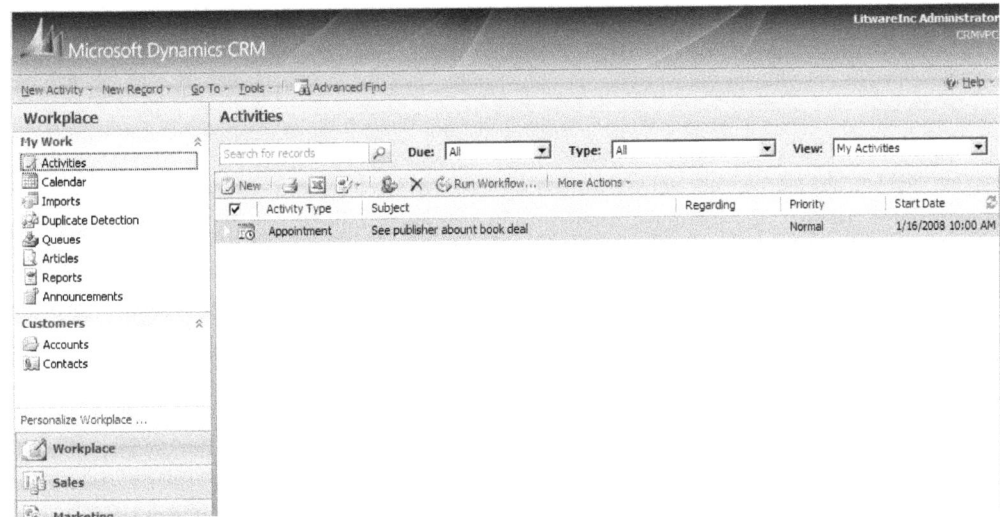

The workplace navigation pane is divided into two with the **My Work** area (described below) and the **customers** area allowing access to **accounts** and **contacts** (leads are available in the sales section). You can also select the **Personalise Workspace** option to bring up the user settings for CRM also available from the **tools-options** menu.

The **My Work** area has the following options:

- **Activities** to view tasks, appointments, emails, and so forth owned by the current user or colleagues or still in a queue (see the activities chapter).
- A **calendar** showing appointments and scheduled activities for the current user (there is a more sophisticated calendar in the service area).
- **Imports** shows the current status and history of bulk imports (see the data management chapter).
- **Duplicate Detection** helps identify and resolve duplicate records imports (see the data management chapter).
- **Queues** are used to receive incoming emails and as a collective area for assigning activities (especially cases) that have yet to be assigned a specific owner.
- **Articles** are available from the knowledge base (see the services chapter).
- **Reports** providing access to reports and the ability to create and edit reports or change the default filter criteria.
- **Announcements** showing the latest news.

9.1. Calendar

The workplace **calendar** shows appointments and service activities for the current user and provides a monthly, weekly, or daily view. You can also add new appointments and service activities from here.

There is a more sophisticated calendar (which shows other users and resources) in the Service work area and you should note that appointments, service activities, tasks, and some other activities may be synchronised with Exchange and viewed from your Outlook client independently of CRM.

Note: There are third party applications available to provide better calendar views from CRM data.

9.2. Queues

Assigning ownership of an activity to a user will add the activity to the **Assigned Queue** so the user can view newly assigned activities, select them and click the **Accept** button to take on ownership of the activity and move it to the **In Progress** queue.

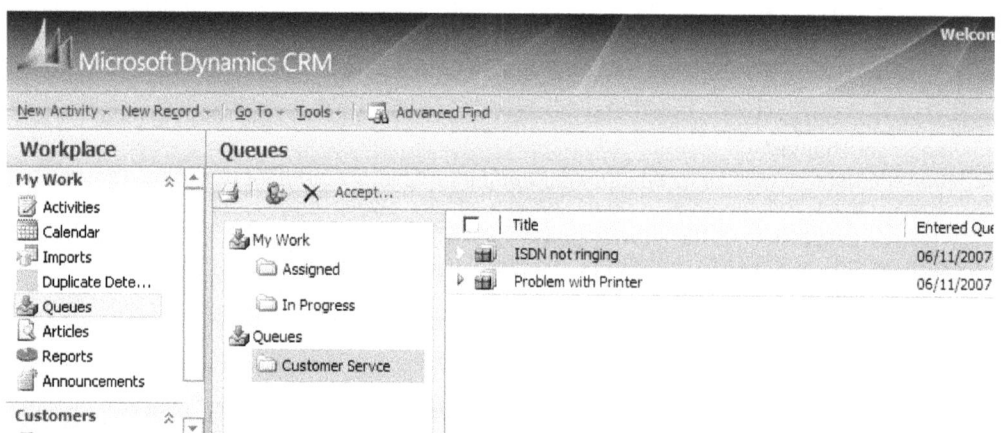

A queue is often set up to accept emails from customers directly from a customer support email address (the CRM Email Router automatically copies the incoming emails into the appropriate queue).

46 Microsoft CRM 4.0 User Handbook

Ownership of a new incoming email can be allocated by workflow rules or selected users instructed to browse the queue and **assign** items to themselves or other users. Automatically allocated emails initially join the **Assigned** queue of the user and can be progressed normally as each user accepts the activities assigned to them. Occasionally the user might return the item back to the queue or assign it to another user.

Note: *Queues are an integral part of working with the service functionality of CRM.*

Activities (including incoming emails) can be **converted** to a **lead**, **opportunity** or a **case** using the appropriate toolbar button or option from the action menu. This will automatically **complete the activity** and further action might begin if appropriate **workflow** is set up to create new activities as old ones are completed.

9.3. Announcements

Announcements are used to show the latest news and new items can be easily added (by users with the appropriate permissions) using the **settings-administration-announcements** form.

Each announcement has a deactivation date and you can set the announcements to be the default page as the user starts up CRM each morning to make sure that new messages are viewed.

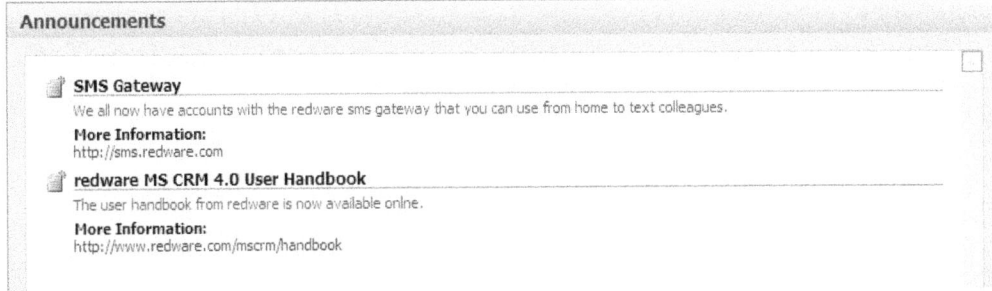

9.4. Personalise Workplace

The personalise workplace option allows you to define your user settings.

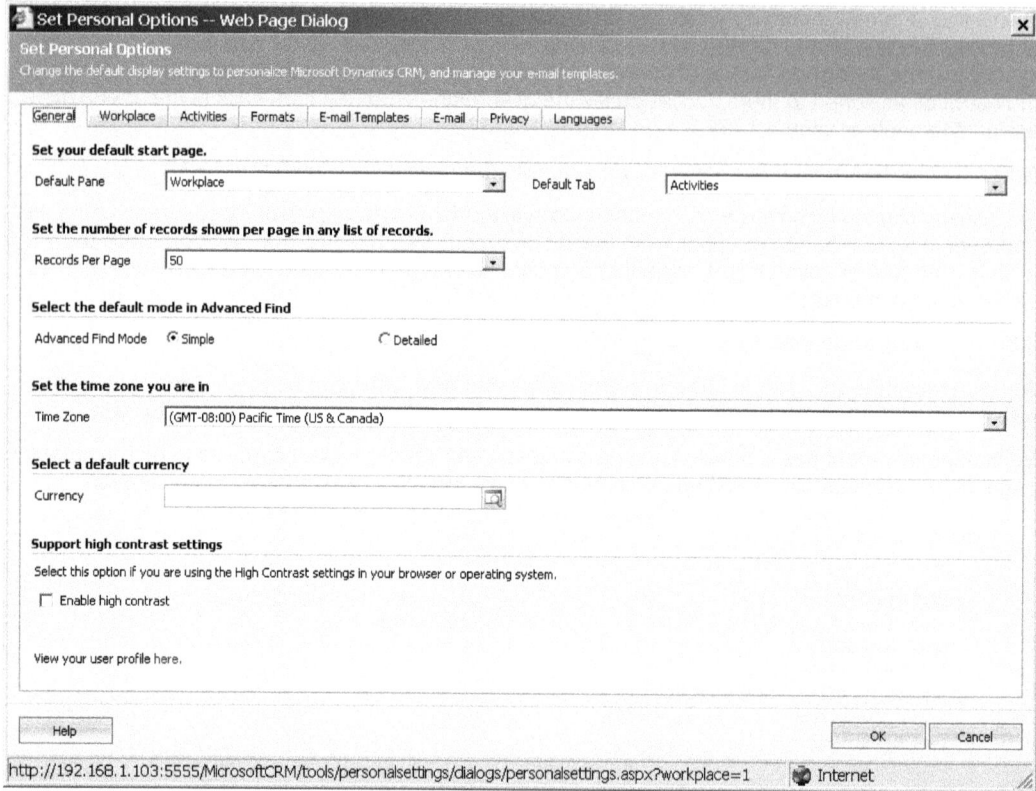

Many features are available:

- **Number of records** to be shown in a View.
- **Default Currency**.
- Default **work area** and pane.
- **Time zone** and default currency.
- **Work hours**.
- **Regional formatting** characteristics for date and decimal formatting.
- **Personal Email templates**.
- **Email synchronisation** settings for Exchange integration.
- Preferred user interface **language**.

Note: Some of these options are also available in the Outlook Client for CRM together with additional options to control the synchronisation process (see the section on the Outlook Client).

10. Products

The **product catalog** is read-only when accessed from the Sales work area and is maintained in the **settings-product catalog** work area.

Products require a short code **product identifier** and a one-line **product name** along with the **unit group** and **default unit item** and the **decimals supported** value. The **default currency** can be specified, and the **price list item** then needs to be added before the product is available for use in the sales cycle.

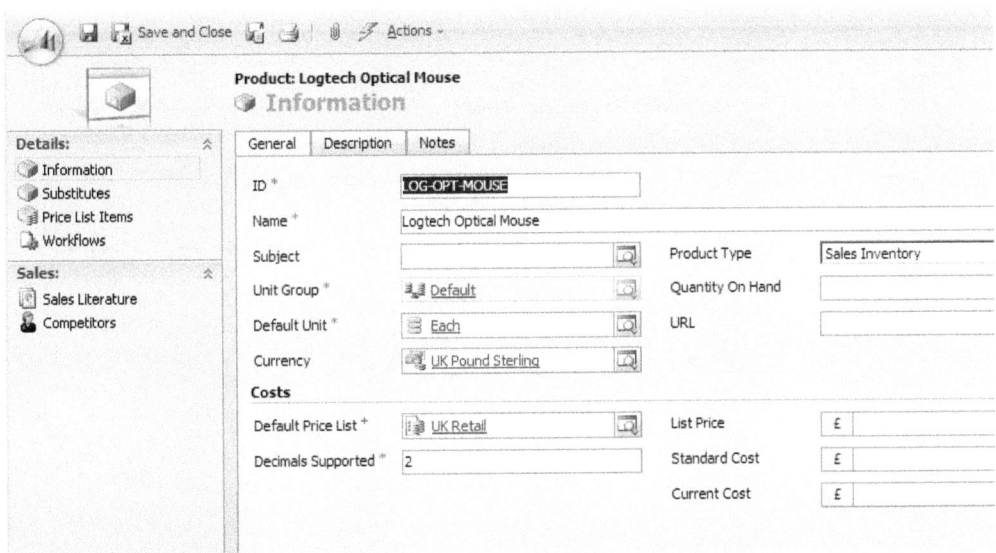

A **price list item** record must be created (for each currency) before a product is available to the sales process. The **list price** and **standard and current cost** are specified in the product record and can be inherited by the price list item records so that a change in the list price would also change all the corresponding price list item records. You can set the **default price list** for a product once the corresponding price list item has been created.

Substitute products can be indicated against a product record and links made to the **sales literature** and **competitor** entities. Products can also be defined as **Product Kits** by selecting the **Convert to Product Kit** option in the actions menu. A kit has several constituent products to form a **bill of materials**.

Note: The author has developed a program to assist in uploading products into CRM from a spreadsheet or accounts package. See http://www.redware.com/mscrm.

10.1. Unit Groups and Items

Unit Groups and **Unit Items** need to be defined before products can be added into the system.

Unit Groups are designed to reflect categories of measurement, so liquids, for example, might have a unit of one millilitre as the smallest **primary unit**. Unit Items are multiples of the primary unit, and a unit of one litre might then be defined for liquids. For whole items, a primary unit for a single unit (each) must be defined and other unit items derived from it with tens and perhaps a dozen or a gross defined for multiples of whole units if required.

Each product must have a **default unit item** taken from a **unit group** that specifies the available unit items permissible for the product.

10.2. Price List Items

The **price list item** specifies the pricing of a **product**, for a particular **pricelist** (and currency) and **unit item**. Once entered, the product is available in the sales cycle (for the appropriate currency only) and the **default pricelist** can be set against the product.

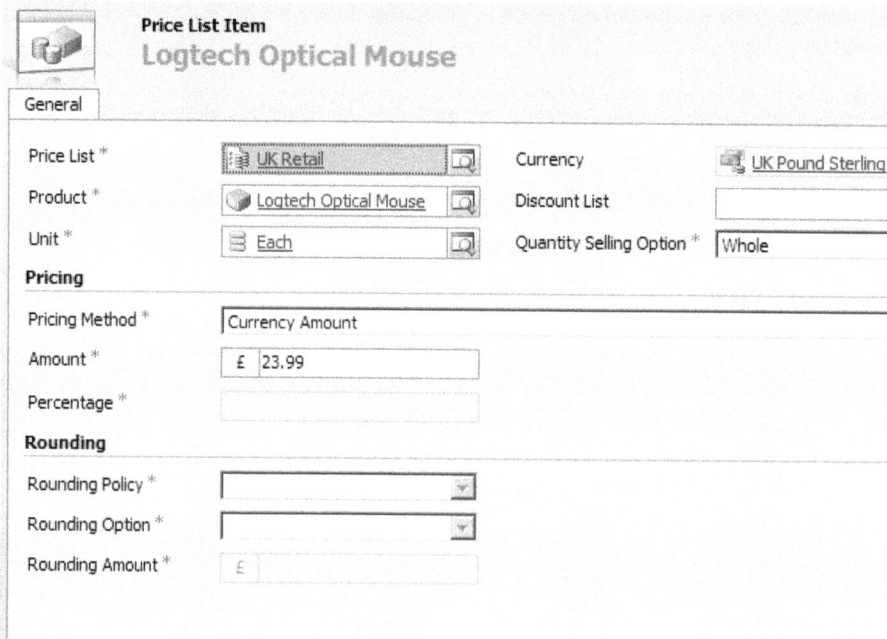

The pricing method allows the price to be inherited from the prices entered against the product or for a specific currency amount defined for each price list item:

- **Currency amount** specifies a precise amount for the price list item with no inheritance from the product record.
- A **percentage of the list price** can be specified so changes to the product price list are automatically reflected in the price list item.
- A **percentage markup or margin** can be specified on either the **standard** or the **current cost** of the product and is automatically updated when the product costs are changed.

Note: *It can be time consuming to maintain price lists with precise currency amounts and you might want to automate the process or at least use the export and import facilities of CRM to maintain prices in a spreadsheet.*

10.3. Discount Lists

Discount lists can be defined to provide discounts according to the quantity ordered. A trade discount list might, for example, apply a 10% discount if more than 100 items are ordered. The discount list can be referenced for each price list term to apply quantity discounts automatically onto a quotation.

**Discount
Information**

General	
Begin Quantity *	10.00000
End Quantity *	25.00000
Percentage *	10.00000

11. Sales

Microsoft has implemented a sophisticated set of features for managing the sales cycle within CRM. The basic premise is that a large number of unqualified **leads** are subjected to a series of marketing **campaigns** and workflow **activities** until the point where they qualify as a sales **opportunity**. At this point, the original lead record is **qualified** and promoted by converting it to a **customer** record (an **account** and/or **contact**) with an associated **opportunity** record.

Opportunities relate to a **customer** record, which can be either an account or a contact record depending on the nature of the business. Potential new business for an existing customer or prospect is recorded by creating a new opportunity against the customer record.

Information on the **products** that interest the prospect are stored against the opportunity together with a **value** and **estimated close date** for the deal. Products and prices are maintained in the **product catalog** (see the Products section) and the users can set the pricing for each item or let the system calculate pricing.

The products held against an opportunity are carried through the sales process as the opportunity is converted into a **quotation**, then an **order**, and finally an **invoice**. **Discounts** and **write-in products** (that are not picked from the product catalog) can be added from the quotation stage onwards (together with sales tax) and **freight costs** can be added at the order stage.

Sophisticated **sales workflow** involving a series of **pipeline phases** can be defined against the opportunity to ensure that the sales pipeline is progressing smoothly. These phases are created with workflow and are similar to workflow stages (see the section on workflow).

The sales cycle involves several entities:

- A **lead** is an unqualified marketing contact.
- An **opportunity** is a qualified sales opportunity associated with a potential **customer** together with associated **products**.
- An **account** represents the company details for a potential customer.
- A **contact** represents the contact details of a company but may also be a customer for consumer sales.

Products can be attached to the opportunity record initially and follow the sales process through as additional entities become involved:

- **Opportunities** have associated products with pricing taken from an appropriate price list and perhaps have a discount applied.
- **Quotations** are created with associated **product items** against a customer usually by converting an opportunity. A quotation can have user pricing to **override** the product pricelist pricing and also **write-in products** that are not attached to any record in the product catalog. **Discounts** and **freight** can also be applied here..
- **Orders** and associated **products** are usually created by converting an active quotation.
- **Invoices** can be created by converting an order although many CRM implementations leave invoices to be extracted from the accounting system.

Activities and **workflow** can be defined against any of these entities although CRM is designed to use the opportunity sales pipeline for monitoring and progressing the sales cycle. One area of systems analysis for CRM installations is the determination of the best practice for storing notes and activities consistently against the different entities associated with each potential sale.

Note: *Some organisations do not require the opportunity phase in the sales cycle and progress directly from a lead to a completed sale.*

The value of the **pipeline phase** for each opportunity is often used in conjunction with the expected date, value, and probability to drive the sales pipeline reports. See the workflow section for a description of how this can be automated.

11.1. Leads

Leads represent contacts at a stage before they become serious sales prospects.

Leads can be created in CRM from a text file using the **bulk import** facility and associated with a **marketing list**. The bulk import feature is discussed in the chapter on data management.

A **quick campaign** (see the marketing chapter) can rapidly create **activities** for organising sales activities such as scheduling outbound phone calls or emails or sales literature fulfilment via a mail merge.

At some point the status of the lead is updated and the lead may be **promoted** to an **opportunity** at which point an associated **customer** (account or contact or both) record is created and the lead is **deactivated** and made read-only.

Note: Deactivated leads can be **reactivated** from the actions menu.

Lead: Fred Bloggs
Information

| General | Details | Administration | Notes |

Address

Street 1	104 Tamworth Road	State/Province	East Sussex
Street 2		ZIP/Postal Code	BN3 5FH
Street 3		Country/Region	England
City	Hove		

Company Information

| Annual Revenue | £ 135,000.00 | SIC Code | 7220 |
| No. of Employees | 4 | Industry | Consulting |

Lead Information

| Lead Source | Trade Show |

There are several predefined fields in the default CRM database used for profiling leads, including **annual revenue**, **industry type** and **lead source**. New attributes can easily be added to the lead entity and the validation set so that values must be entered by the user when a new lead is created. This can help in analysing the success of marketing efforts and is recommended practice.

Note: You should make sure that your system customiser defines mappings for additional fields created for a lead so that these values are copied automatically to the appropriate contact or account entity when the lead is qualified and the new records created.

Leads are converted to Opportunities (or disqualified) using the **Convert Lead** button on the form menu. The lead can be converted to the corresponding new account, contact and opportunity records or converted to a new opportunity against an existing customer record.

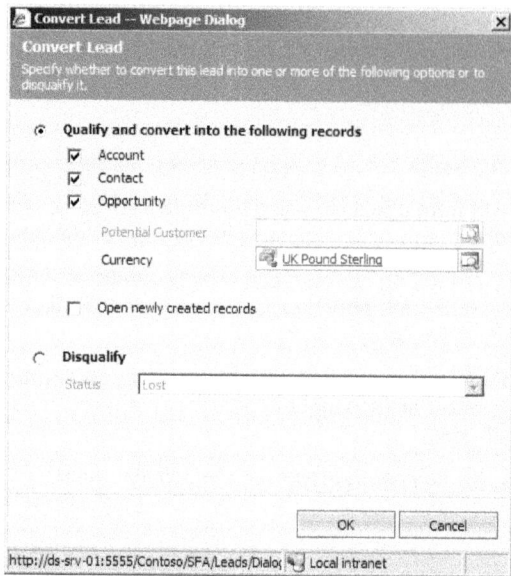

Qualified leads are deactivated (made read-only) in the database and converted to the corresponding customer and opportunity records. A link to the original lead is available from the opportunity entity to trace back over the history if required.

Leads that fail to progress through to the sales pipeline can be **disqualified** rather than **deleted**. This means that the data is available for analysis later.

11.2. Opportunities

Opportunities are integral to monitoring the sales pipeline and represent a business opportunity with a customer or a prospect (either an account or a contact record). Leads must be converted to an opportunity before they are considered part of the sales pipeline.

Note: *Some users of sales and marketing systems such as Act! And Goldmine find it difficult to move from one view of data to having data stored for a single prospect in the lead, account, contact, and opportunity entities (not to mention the related activities).*

The key fields for the opportunity are the **potential customer**, the **currency**, and the **pricelist**. Each user has a **default currency** which is set into the lead initially and is carried through to the customer and opportunity when the lead is converted. The currency cannot be changed once the opportunity has been created and determines the available pricelists that can be selected.

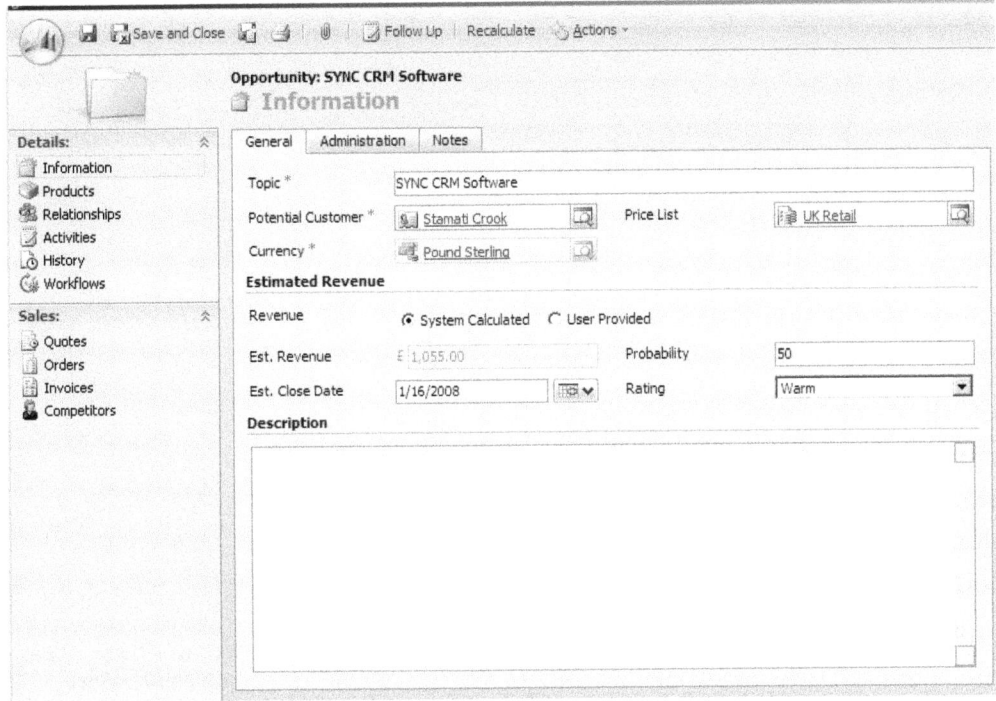

Note: New opportunities are created for existing customers to represent a new piece of potential business.

Once the price list has been specified, **products** may be added to the opportunity to reflect the interests of the potential customer. The individual products linked to an opportunity must come from a **product price list item**.

Prices are specified for each **product** against a **pricelist** (for each currency) and a base **unit** which must be specified together with the quantity and price. The options to alter prices and add discounts depend on the specification of the product and the user's security settings.

Note: Write-in products that do not derive from the price lists and discounts can be added at the quotation stage.

Prices are automatically calculated for **system calculated** opportunities which will automatically reflect any price changes made to the product price list items when the **recalculate** option is selected.

User provided prices can be set if the user has the appropriate security permissions and should be used when a firm price is given to the customer as they do not change automatically when recalculated.

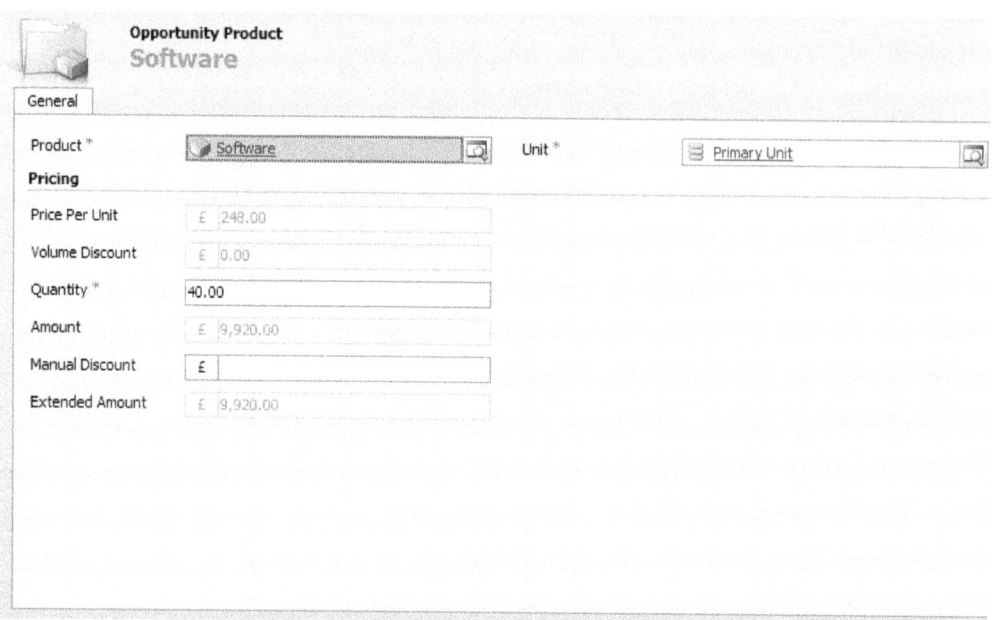

Note: Clicking on the product hyperlink will bring up the relevant product form which shows the standard retail and cost prices and links through to **competitor and sales literature** information as well as all the price list items for that product.

The **sales pipeline** value is determined by the **probability** and the **estimated revenue** and **close date** and is an important management figure. **Pipeline phases** (see the workflow section) can be specified to monitor the sales process by automatically assigning a probability at different stages to reflect the business processes surrounding the sales pipeline.

11.3. Quotations

A new quotation is made by selecting the quotations pane from the opportunity record and creating a new quotation. This automatically copies the products already associated with the opportunity into the quotation.

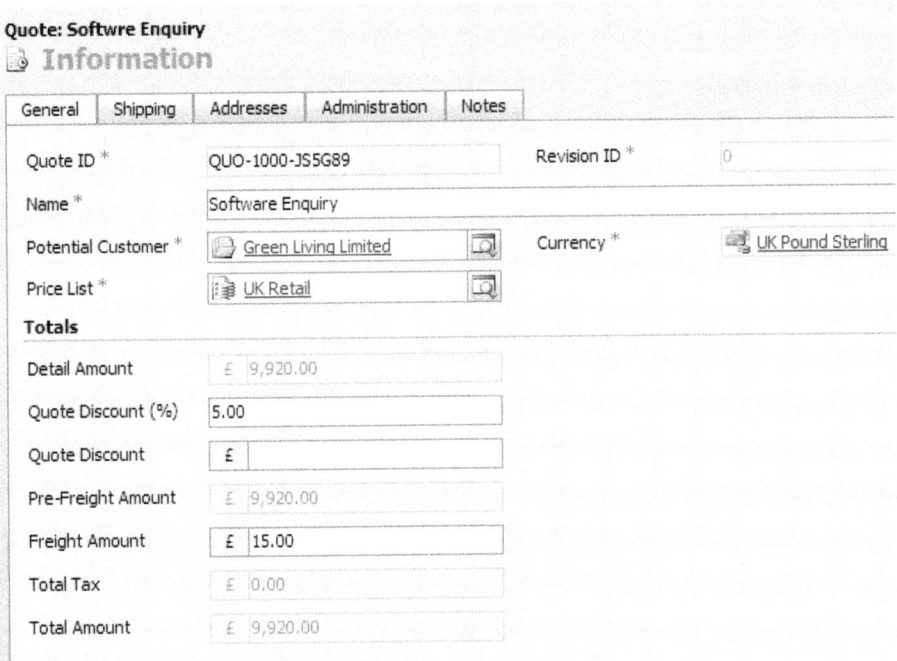

A **discount percentage** and **freight charges** can be added at this stage if required. The expected delivery dates and the shipping and invoice addresses are set in the **shipping** and **addresses** tabs of the form.

The pricing information stored against the quotation products can be changed and **write-in products** added that do not use the existing product codes or pricelists. You can specify the **override price** option to set your own price for a product item so that it is not changed (when the price is **recalculated**) because of a change to the product price list item.

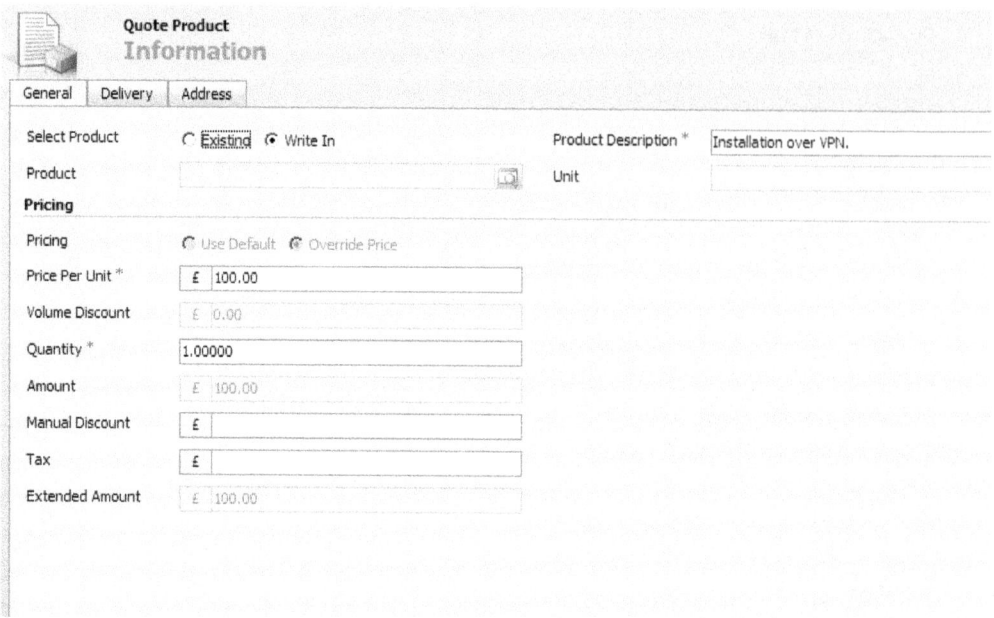

Note: Most installations will want to implement a JavaScript solution on the form for the tax calculation which does not seem to be built in to CRM (see the customisation chapter).

Once the Quotation is complete you should use the option on the Actions menu to **Activate Quote**.

Use the **Print Quote for Customer** button to merge the quotation to Word, by means of your quotation Word template which can be stored in CRM. You can then distribute the document to the prospect (remembering to append a copy of the document as a file attached to the quotation in the notes field).

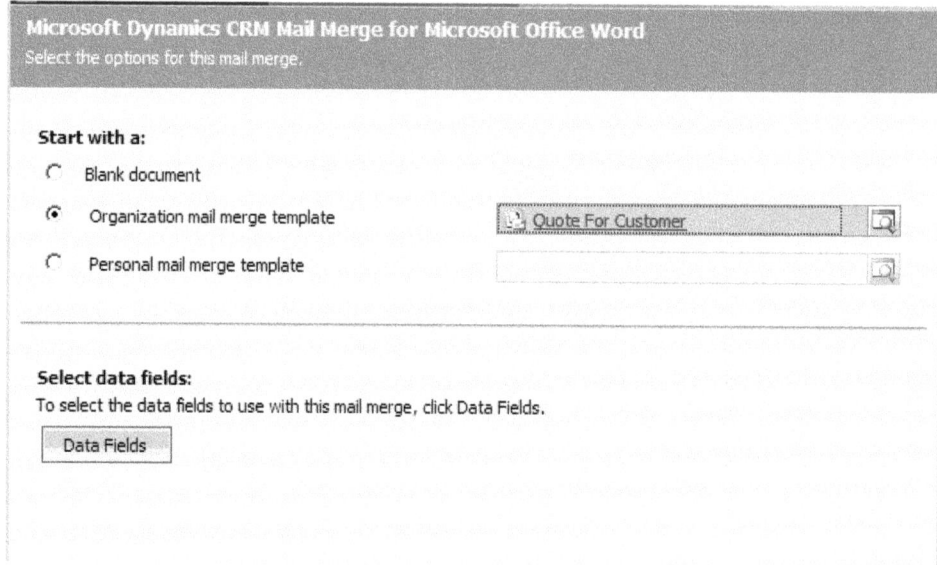

Additional options on the Actions menu allow you to **get products**, perhaps from an opportunity created for another customer, or **lookup addresses** to specify the delivery and invoice addresses.

A **version number** is applied to each Quotation and best practice is to **activate** the quotation before sending to the prospect. Select the **revise quote** option from the Actions if you need to modify an existing quote and note that the **revision ID** for the quotation has been incremented.

The actions menu provides the **create order** option to convert the Quotation to an **order** (the quotation must be activated before it can be converted) if the quotation is accepted by the customer. On the other hand, if the quotation is not accepted, use the **close quote** option to indicate that the sale has been lost and indicate the appropriate reasons.

11.4. Orders

Orders have functionality similar to that of Quotations and allow modification of the final order information if required.

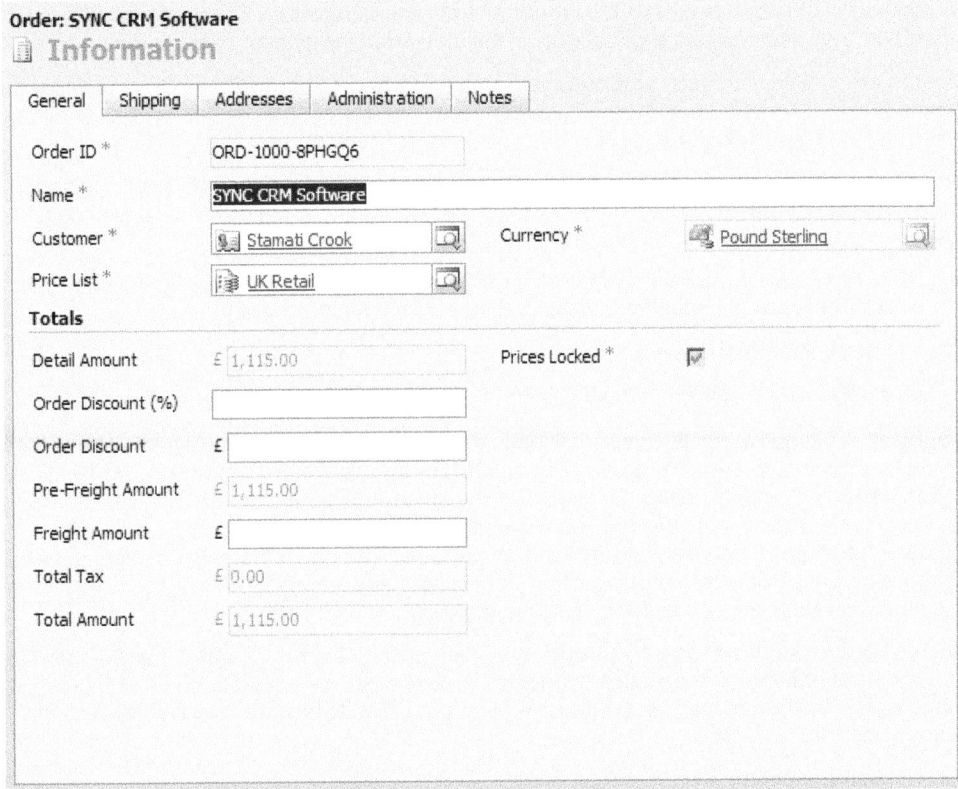

The action menu is used to **fulfil** an order when it is complete and needs to be dispatched to the customer. Alternatively, the order might be **cancelled** (and the appropriate reason entered) or simply **deleted**.

Other options available for an order include looking up **addresses** and **recalculating** or using the **current product pricing** from the appropriate pricelists.

Finally, an **Invoice** can be created from the fulfilled Order record. Some of the accounts integration products stop invoices from being created within CRM and take completed orders to add into the accounting package and then copy the invoices back into CRM.

Note: *The author has such software available for Sage and QuickBooks at http://www.redware.com/mscrm and Microsoft have their own offering for Dynamics accounting software.*

11.5. Invoices

Invoices allow recalculation of the pricing information using the latest product pricing and can be **cancelled** or **deleted**. The actions menu allows the status to change to **Invoice Paid** which completes the Invoice so that it can no longer be updated.

Note: *Many installations make invoices read-only and use their accounting system as the source of invoicing data. Take some care if you use invoices as multiple Invoices can be created from a single order. You may need to print invoices with a custom report and remember that Invoices should not be updatable once they have been dispatched to the customer.*

11.6. Currency

Each user and customer has a default currency and all monetary values are stored against a specified currency together with a calculation of the amount in the system base currency.

Currencies are maintained in the **settings-business management-currencies** area and allow an exchange rate to be entered against the base currency. The current figures can be maintained by uploading a file of the latest currency rates.

Only the current prices are maintained and it is important to understand that the base currency values stored against each currency amount are recalculated only when any money field on a record is changed or the status for that record is changed.

Note: *The base currency for the installation is set during the installation process but the system customiser can change the name and symbol of the base currency.*

11.7. Sales Administration

Additional entities play a role in the organisation of the sales process in CRM:

- **Subject**. A hierarchy of subjects is defined in the **settings-business management-subjects** area to allow a consistent hierarchy to be applied for organising products and sales literature.
- **Competitors**. Competitors can be defined in the **sales-competitors** area with links to the products they supply and notes on their strengths and weaknesses.
- **Sales Literature**. A set of documents can be uploaded into the **sales-sales literature** area and tracked against products and competitors. An abstract and keywords help in searching for the required literature where there are many related products involved.

Sales Territories can be defined and allocated against each customer. Territories are created in the **system-business management-sales territories** area and have a manager and a number of member users. Each Customer can be assigned to a particular Territory allowing sales pipeline analysis by territory (and territory manager).

11.8. Sales Pipeline

The **sales pipeline** is an essential tool for sales and marketing management and shows the predicted level of orders currently coming through the sales process.

Sales pipeline reports (from the **workplace-reports** pane) use the opportunity data (comprising the probability, estimated value and estimated close date) to predict sales forecasts against the salesperson, business unit, territory and so on. Take a look at other reports regarding the sales pipeline including the **Sales History**, **Sales Pipeline** and **Neglected Leads** reports.

11.9. Sales Quotas

Sales quotas can be set against each user from the **actions-manage quotas** option of the user form. This option only appears after the fiscal year has been defined for the CRM installation.

Note: *The fiscal year settings cannot be changed once they have been set so take great care to decide if you want monthly, quarterly, or annual sales quotas and take a backup before setting this value into the system.*

Sales quotas are entered by selecting the fiscal period and currency and simply entering the sales targets for each user. These are then used in the pipeline reports.

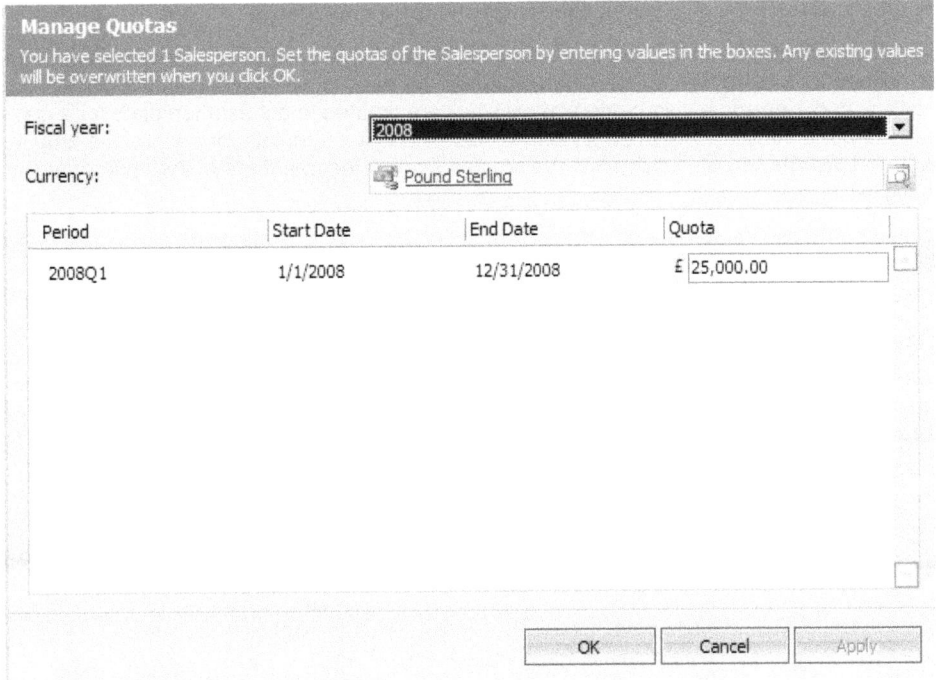

12. Marketing

Marketing is designed to aid the conversion of **leads** into **opportunities** by creating the appropriate **activities** to manage processes for a marketing campaign such as the mailing of a letter or the making of an outbound sales call to the lead. Marketing also applies to customer retention and cross-selling campaigns focussing on **existing customers** or prospects.

Marketing Lists are an important organisational feature of CRM which can be applied to many different business processes. These lists are a collection of leads, accounts or contacts that can be created manually or in accordance with any possible filter criteria. Marketing lists can be used to quickly **create activities** with **a quick campaign** and run **a mail merge** to Word.

Marketing lists are also used to drive a full marketing **campaign**. A series of **campaign activities** can be defined for a campaign to act as templates for generating activities against a collection of mailing lists. In our example, two campaign activities are created to act as a template for a mailshot and a follow-up call activity. A campaign activity is created as a template for each of the required activities and **distributed** as activity records created against the members of the appropriate marketing list.

Associated **costs** can be summated for each campaign by looking at the costs associated with each distributed activity. The performance and return on investment can be measured by creating **campaign responses** for each campaign and tracking them against any **opportunities** created.

12.1. Marketing Lists

Marketing Lists can be used to generate successive campaigns or control business processes such as regular mailings or courtesy calls made to customers. Marketing lists are defined for **leads**, **accounts** or **contacts** and consist of little information other than the list of **members**.

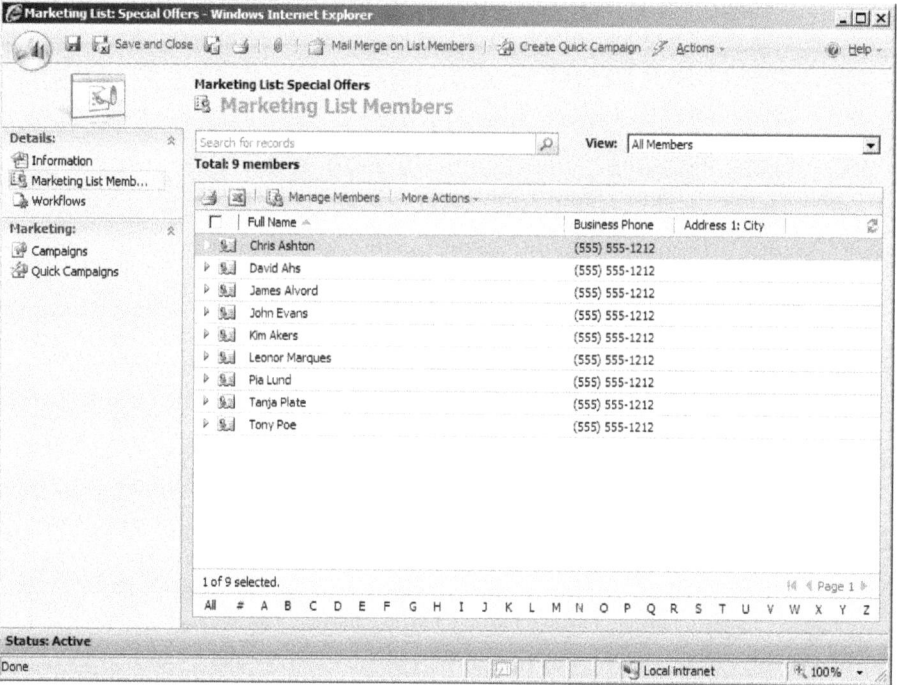

Members can be managed from the marketing list form by selecting the **Manage List Members** form and clicking on the **Manage Members** button, which provides several options to manage members by using the features of advanced find.

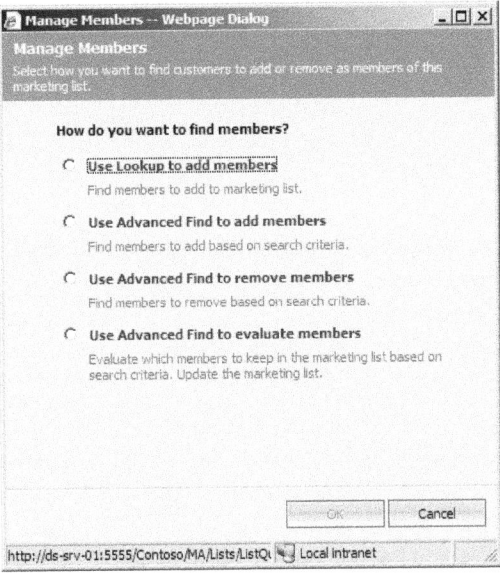

Note: Remember that a filter can be complex and include related entities so that customers (accounts or contacts) can be filtered in accordance with, for example, the products in which they have shown an interest.

The **lookup members** option allows you to define a selection with an advanced find query and add the selected accounts, contacts, or leads into the marketing list. **Add members** will add new members found via the required query into the marketing list and **remove members** will remove members from an existing list in accordance with the query. **Evaluate** keeps only those members already on the marketing list that match the query and discards the remainder.

Marketing Lists can also be useful in situations where the advanced find query is not appropriate for selecting the required data. In this case, a marketing list can be created by manually adding the entity occurrences to the list. The contact, account and lead forms allow individual records to be added or removed from marketing lists with the **add to marketing list** button so a salesperson can create their own marketing lists.

Marketing Lists can also be created automatically when performing a **bulk import** from a spreadsheet file to create, for example, a marketing list for a tradeshow.

Mail merging to Word is available from the toolbar of a marketing list and creates a mail merge file integrated with Word for creating letters, envelopes, faxes, labels and also emails directly from Outlook (see the Using CRM section).

Quick Campaigns (see the Using CRM section) can quickly generate activities for a marketing list but campaign activities (see below) offer a more sophisticated approach.

12.2. Campaigns

Campaigns are used to help plan and organise marketing campaigns and keep track of costs and return on investment. A campaign is created from the **marketing-campaigns** work area and specifies basic campaign details, including the **price list**, the proposed and actual **start** and **end** dates and a **budget** and estimated **revenue** (on the financials page).

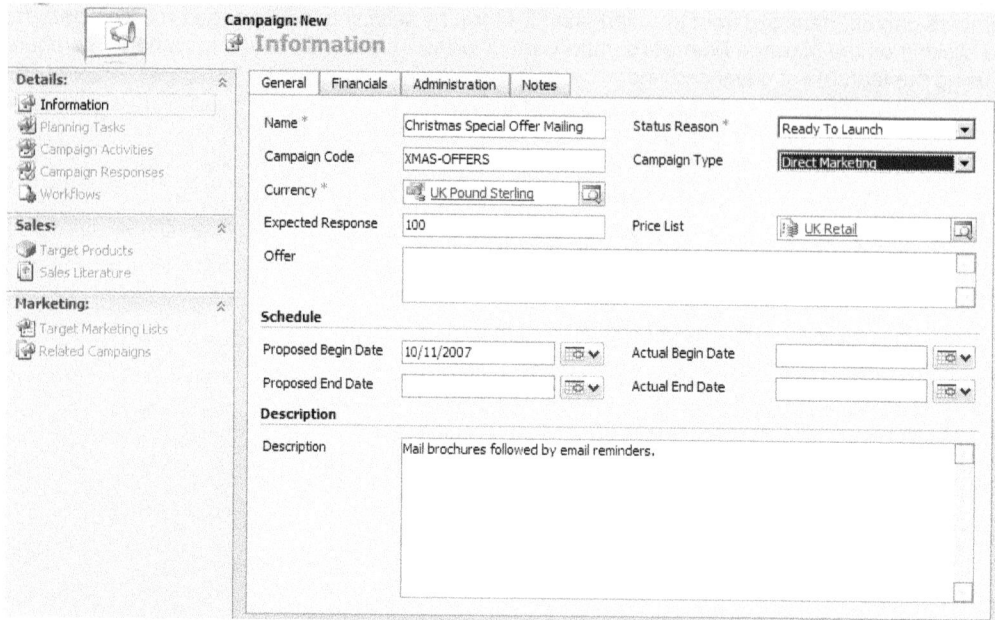

The **Expected Response** refers to the percentage of campaign responses expected from the activities performed. The **Target Products** and **Sales Literature** panes are for reference only and provide users with quick access to relevant information when dealing with a campaign response. **Related Campaigns** may also be of interest to the Marketing department (perhaps for reporting purposes).

The **planning tasks** pane is a quick method of adding **tasks** to the current campaign to represent the planning and preparation process. These tasks do not affect the campaign in any way and are just a convenient place to view the various tasks associated with a campaign.

Several pre-built reports are available to monitor campaigns including the **Campaign Performance** report available from the campaign form and the **Campaign Activity Status and Campaign Comparison** report available from the **workspace-reports** area

12.3. Campaign Activities

Campaign Activities are templates used to generate activities related to a campaign against the members of the marketing lists associated with the campaign.

A new campaign activity is defined and a **channel** selected to indicate the type of marketing activity (letter, fax, email and so forth). The activities are then **distributed** and recorded as activities within CRM. Later these activities are converted to campaign **responses** so that the success of the campaign can be monitored.

Campaign Activity: Send Brochure by Mail

Parent Campaign *	Christmas Special
Channel	Letter via Mail Merge
Subject *	Send Brochure by Mail
	Cover letter and brochure to be sent second class postage.
Status Reason	Proposed
Type	Direct Follow-Up Contact
Owner *	CRM Admin
Outsource Vendors	redware research ltd; Carol Phillips
Scheduled Start	15/11/2007
Scheduled End	22/11/2007
Budget Allocated	£ 175.00
Priority	High
Actual Start	
Actual End	
Actual Cost	£ 220.00

Anti-Spam Setting: Exclude marketing list members if contacted within set time period

No. of Days	0

Each activity generated can have an associated **budget** and **cost** which are summated on the campaign activity form and could also be used to help manage **outsourced vendors** (external suppliers).

The **channel** is the most important setting on the campaign activity and is used to generate **activities** according to the **marketing lists** attached to the campaign. The available channels comprise:

- **Phone.**
- **Appointment.**
- **Letter.**
- **Letter via Mail Merge** which uses the Outlook CRM client.
- **Fax.**
- **Fax by Mail Merge** which uses the Outlook CRM client.
- **Email.**
- **Email via Mail Merge** which uses the Outlook CRM client.
- **Other.**

The **Distribute Campaign Activities** button appears once the campaign activities form has been saved and brings up a form template to create the appropriate activity record for each entity occurrence in the campaign marketing lists. You can control the ownership of the created activities.

Note: *The Anti-Spam Setting excludes records that have been contacted within the specified number of days.*

12.4. Distribute Campaign Activities via Mail Merge (Outlook)

The Outlook client for CRM can be used to distribute letters, faxes, or emails via mail merge and the corresponding activity records can be generated (usually as completed activities) once the mail merge in Word has finished with the following dialog window:

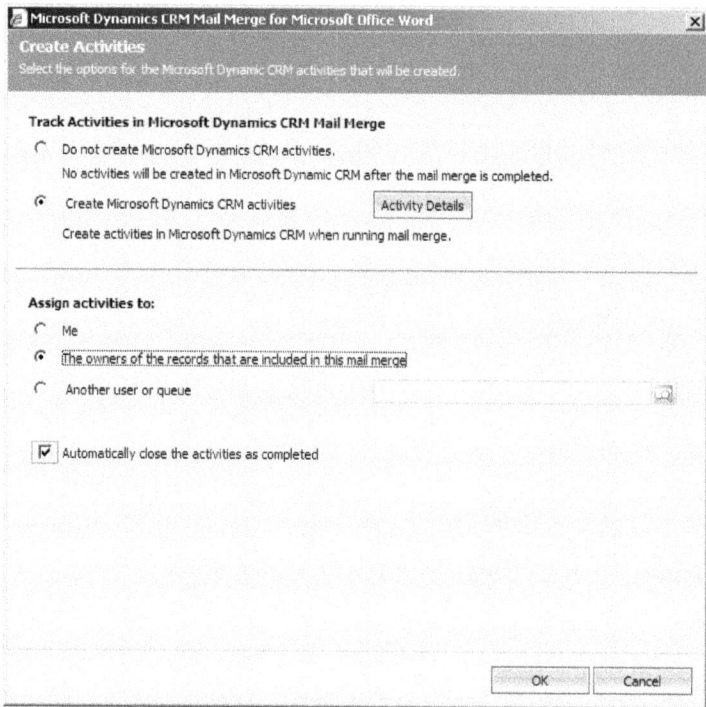

Note: Using the Outlook Client allows you to attach the relevant document to the activity.

12.5. Campaign Templates

You can save time by defining a **campaign template** if you are running a series of similar campaigns. An existing campaign can be **copied to a template** or **copied as a new campaign** from the action menu when looking at the campaign form.

12.6. Campaign Responses

Campaign Responses are used to monitor the activity resulting from a campaign.

Activities created with a campaign have a **Promote to Response** option on the actions menu (this should really be more prominent). Selecting this brings up the campaign response form, which can be used to record additional details required by the marketing department and also drives the reporting to measure the success of the campaign.

Individual activities created for a campaign activity can be viewed in the navigation pane of the campaign form and promoted to a response as required. Campaign activities can also be viewed in the **workplace-activities** area as well as against the corresponding lead, account, or contact record.

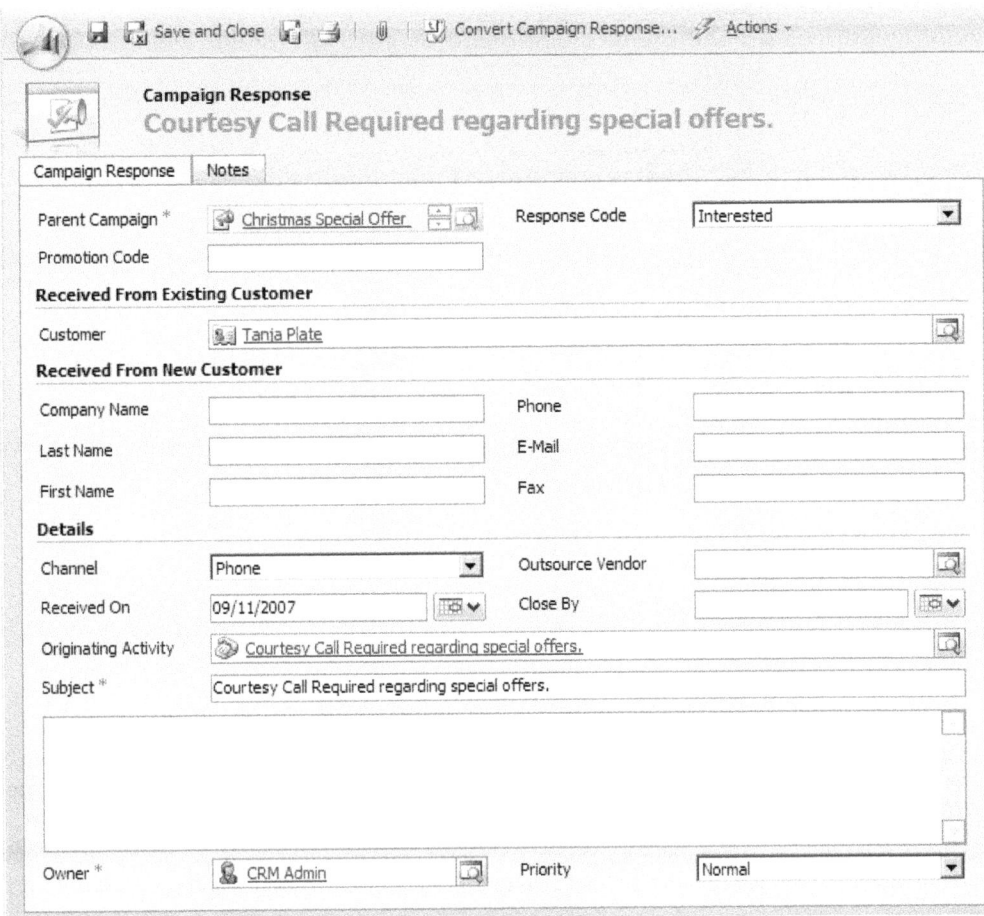

Note: The **outsource vendor** can be used to track reseller or affiliate schemes where an external organisation was responsible for generating the lead.

Emails sent out as part of a campaign can be automatically converted to campaign responses if a reply is received from the target (provided that incoming email and tracking are implemented on your CRM system).

Campaign responses can also be created as a new activity from the **new activity-campaign response** menu as responses to a campaign begin to arrive. Here the **Received from New Customer** details are filled in after the appropriate parent campaign has been selected.

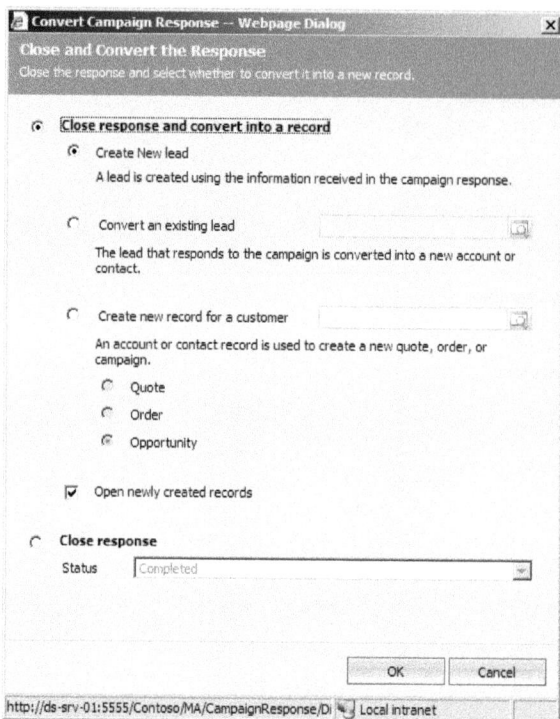

The **Convert Campaign Response** option is made available once a new campaign response record has been saved and this allows the campaign response to be closed and details converted to a **new lead** (for new details), or an **existing lead** to be converted to an account or contact, or for a **new quote**, **order** or **opportunity** to be created for an existing customer.

Close the response and change the status to **disqualified** if the campaign response does not fulfil the campaign requirements.

13. Service

The service area allows you to control the management and resolution of customer support cases as they arrive within CRM. Service queues can be set up easily to receive incoming emails and activities can be converted to a case against a queue. Customer Service staff can then browse the queue and accept cases working towards their resolution. The case can be put back in the queue or assigned to second or third line support if it cannot be resolved.

Service relates to the management and resolution of customer support **cases**. The principal entities involved are as follows:

- **Cases** defined for each customer service incident.
- **Contracts** which may be created against a customer if service contracts are relevant to the organisation and cases tracked against support contracts.
- **Knowledgebase Articles** which allow a rudimentary automated help desk facility where a bank of articles can easily be searched and emailed to resolve a case.
- A **subject** hierarchy for organising the knowledge base and cases.
- **Service Activities** which require the allocation of at least one **resource** to an activity (see the next section).
- **Activities** can be created for a case and must all be completed before the case is resolved.

13.1. Cases

A Case is defined to cope with a customer service enquiry. A case is defined against a **customer** and must have a **title**, an **owner** and a **subject** and must be linked to a **customer**.

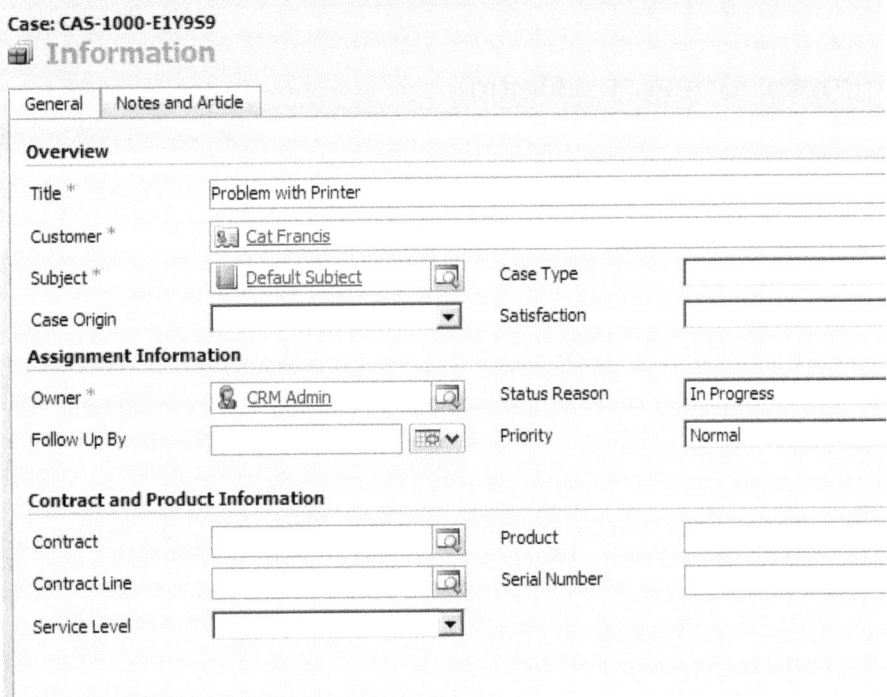

The **Notes and Article** tab is a convenient place to store progress notes against a case but also allows a full text search of the **knowledge base**. If an appropriate knowledge base article is found, it can be stored against the case and easily emailed to the customer.

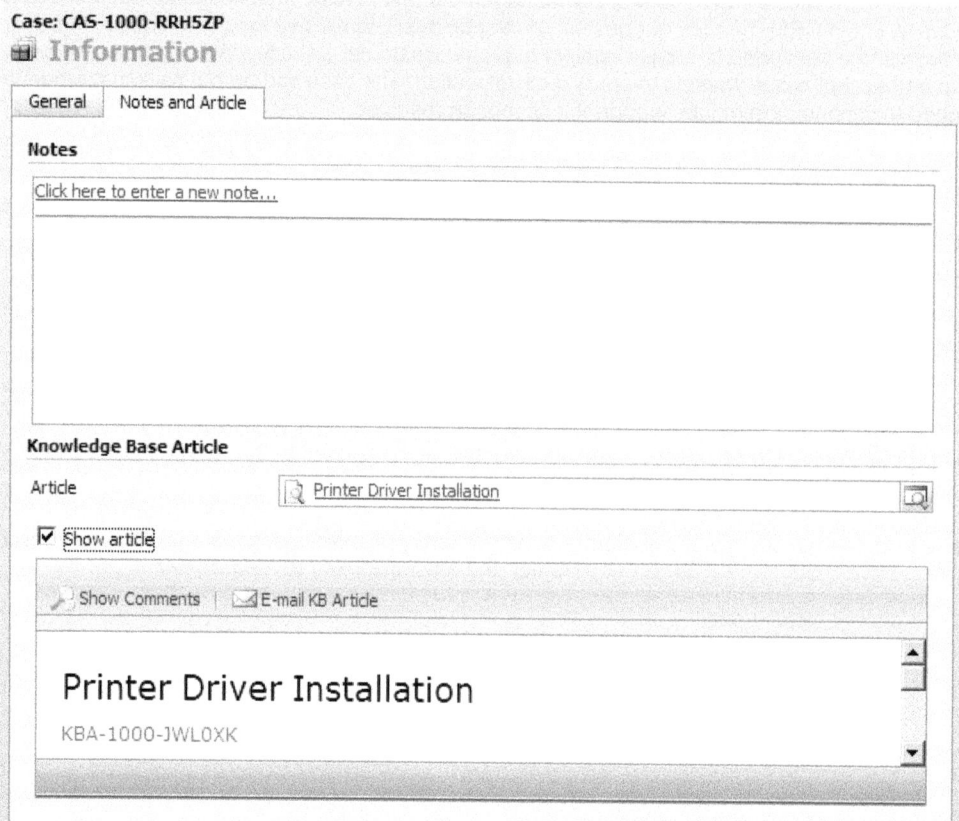

Note: You can email the knowledge base article directly to the customer if you click the **show article** checkbox on the case form and press the **Email KB Article** button.

Cases can be created from the account or contact form and should be attached to a contract if you need to track work done against a customer to match the time spent against the contract limits.

A case can also be created by **converting an activity** to a case from an incoming **email** for example. Some installations have an incoming email address (for example support@redware.com) that brings emails into a queue for the customer service team to view and promote to cases as required.

Queues are an integral part of working with the service functionality of CRM and newly promoted activities or incoming emails from a customer support email or helpdesk activities are often assigned to a queue where the customer service person dealing with the request is not known when the case is created. Members of the customer service team can browse unresolved cases and take ownership to proceed to a resolution. The case can be reassigned back to the queue if the issue cannot be resolved and the case completed.

Incoming cases may be assigned to customer service personnel initially by the first line support team or automatically using workflow. Each customer service representative can view their personal queues in the **workplace-my work** area which shows all newly assigned cases. Newly assigned cases appear in the **assigned** personal queue and move over to the **in progress** queue as each case is accepted (see the workplace section on queues).

Although anyone can view and add activities, only the case owner can **resolve** or **reactivate** a case from the action menu, and cases can only be resolved if all activities held against it have been completed.

13.2. Contract Template

Contract Templates must be set up to provide similar terms and conditions for different service contracts. They can be defined in the **settings-templates-contract templates** work area and determine whether **time** or **number of cases** apply as a constraint on the contract and also set out the available **working hours**.

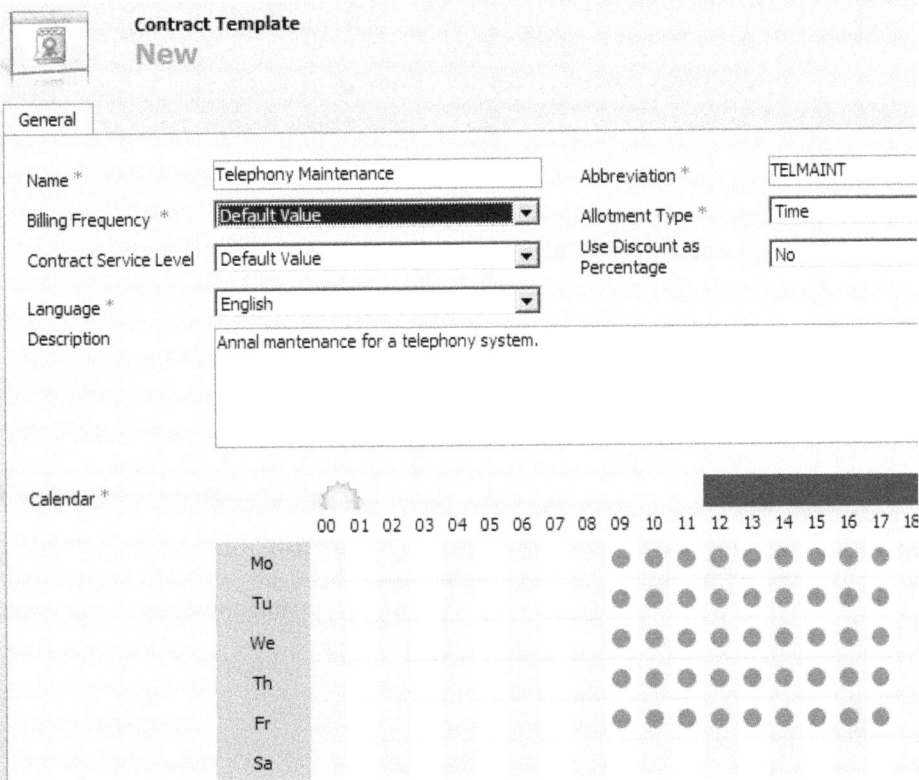

13.3. Contract

Service Contracts are defined against a customer, showing the dates for which service activity is covered. The contract **name** and **customer** together with the **start** date and **end** date of the contract must be specified, along with the **billing address** and **currency**.

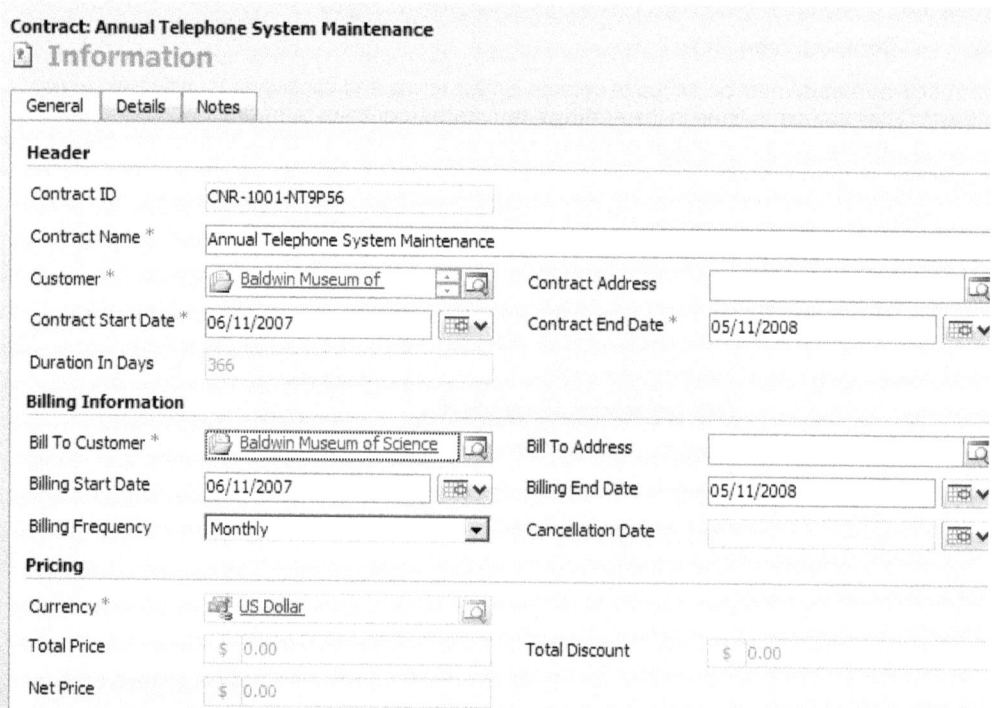

At least one **contract line item** must be added to the Contract before it can be invoiced. The total number of cases or the time allowed for all related activities can be defined on the contact line item and monitored by viewing the **allotments used** and **allotments remaining** fields on the contract line item form.

The contract line item must have a **title** and a **start** and **end** dates and a constraint on the total **time** or number of **cases** allocated as well as a **price**. Contract line items usually refer to an item of equipment related to a **product** record.

Contract Line: Panasonic Telephone System Maintenance

Title *	Panasonic Telephone System Maintenance		
Product		Unit	
Quantity		Location	
Start Date *	06/11/2007	End Date *	05/11/2008

Allotment Details

Total Cases/Minutes *	50
Allotments Used	0
Allotments Remaining	50

Pricing

Total Price *	$ 400.00	Rate	$ 8.00
Discount in (%) or	$ 0.00		
Net	$ 400.00		

A contract is not activated to be used until the **invoice Contract** action has been selected. This does not create an invoice record but makes the contract record **read-only** and allows the contract to be referenced with a case. The contract cannot be activated until at least one contract line item has been added.

Contracts can be put **on hold** (and **released**) and **renewed** if their expiry date is reached. Individual contract line items can be **cancelled**. Renewing a contract will create a new contract with the same details as the original.

Note: *Making the contract read-only after it is invoiced makes it difficult to add further contract line items to the contract while it is in progress and can cause some usability issues.*

The total time and resources available for each contract can be used to check service activity against each contract as shown in the **service management reports**.

13.4. Knowledge Base

The **knowledge base** allows resolutions to common customer service issues to be documented, and one method of resolving a case is to search the knowledge base area and link to the knowledge base article (which can also be emailed easily to the customer).

Users can add **comments** to articles to improve the knowledge base and articles can be associated with a case in the **Notes and Article** tab (or using the form assistant) and added to any email by pressing the **Insert KB Article** form button on the Email form.

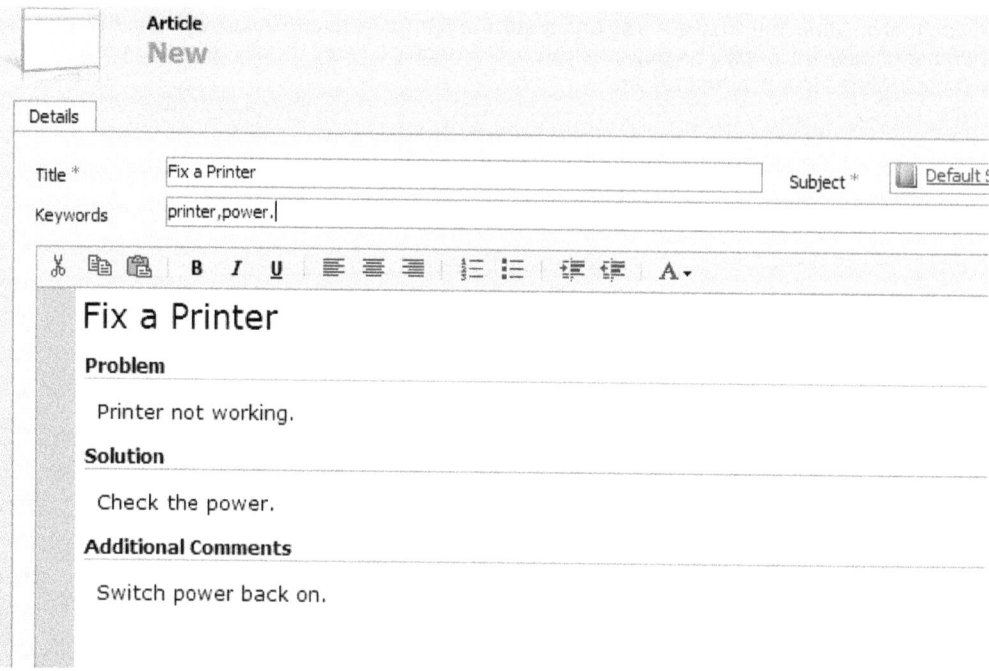

Each article is assigned to a **subject** which is part of a hierarchy to help organise articles (and cases and products) and can be set up in the **settings** area.

An **article template** is required for each article (**settings-templates-article templates**), and users can create articles if they have the appropriate security settings. Once an article has been completed, the **submit** action is required to submit the article for **approval**. Once approved (probably by a manager), the articles can be searched for easily by any user and inserted into emails in addition to being used to resolve a case.

Note: *The knowledge base index is updated every 15 minutes and so changes are not made available immediately.*

14. Scheduling

Scheduling makes it easy to find time slots where all the required resources are available for booking a service activity. Some examples might include:

- Telesales staff need to book a sales person for an appointment with a prospect.
- Dentists might define a service type for a check-up that takes 20 minutes and requires the customer to be allocated an appointment with their preferred dentist.
- An estate agent might have his day chopped into 45 minute slots for showing prospects around to view a property.
- A service engineer might need to visit a customer with some tools and equipment if a case cannot be resolved.

Service activities are similar to appointments in that **multiple resources** can be booked for a particular time and show up on the service **calendar**. Service activities can be used to book **equipment** and **resources,** in addition to **users** and **customers**, and have a **schedule** button available to help identify available times.

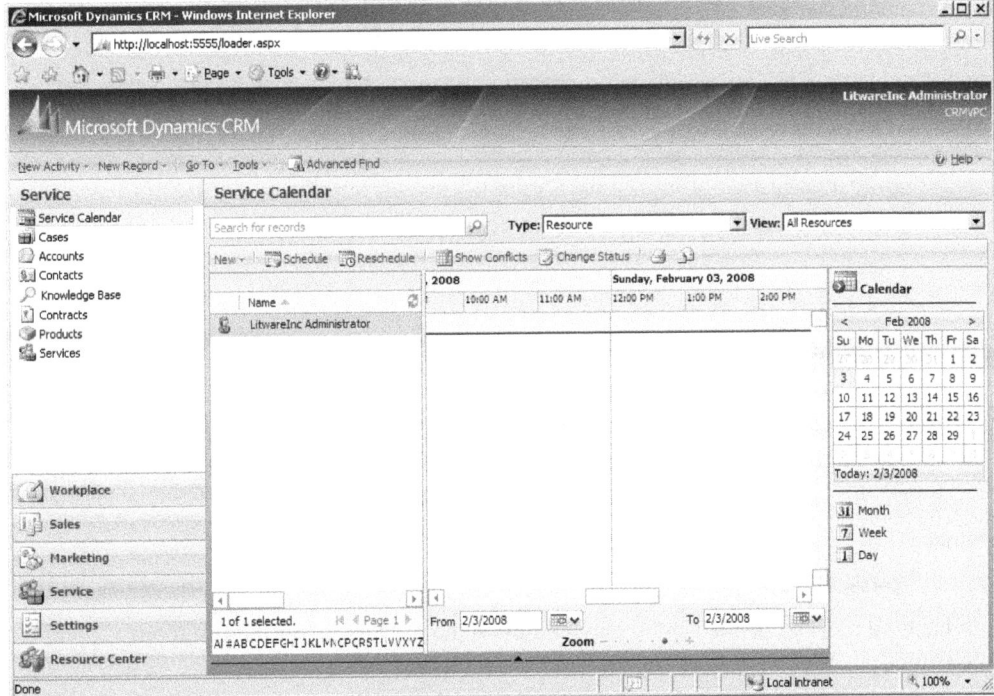

Each service activity must have a **subject** and a **service type** and a **start** and **end** time. The service type indicates the default **duration** of the activity and the **resources** required (see below).

Service Activities can be created manually as for any activity but are often created with a scheduling process which indicates the next available timeslots where all required resources are available to fulfil the service activity.

14.1. Resources and Equipment

Equipment can be defined against a business unit and might represent a **facility** such as a meeting room or a physical item such as an LCD Projector.

Microsoft CRM 4.0 User Handbook   75

Equipment is defined in the settings-business **management-equipment/facilities** area for each **site** and can have an email address and a **time zone**.

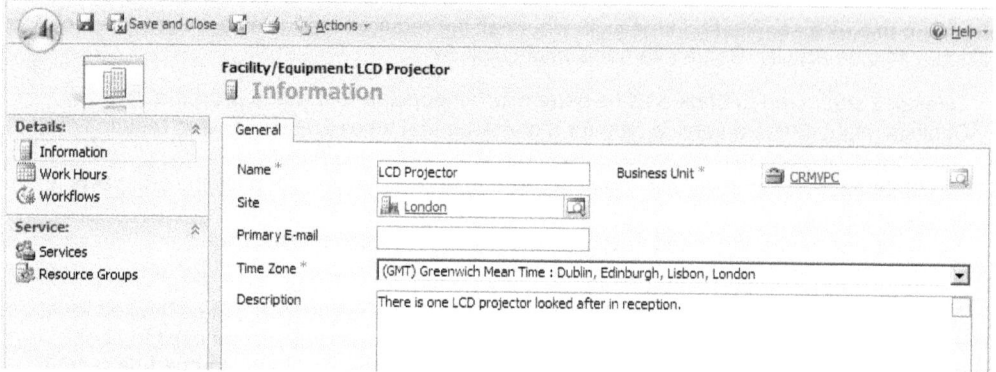

Equipment and facilities can be made available for particular **working hours** and also be defined as located at a particular **site**. The scheduling facility makes use of this data to provide information on resource availability for each site when a new service activity is being created.

Collections of resources can be defined as **resource groups** and are scheduled together and defined in the **settings-business management-resource groups** area:

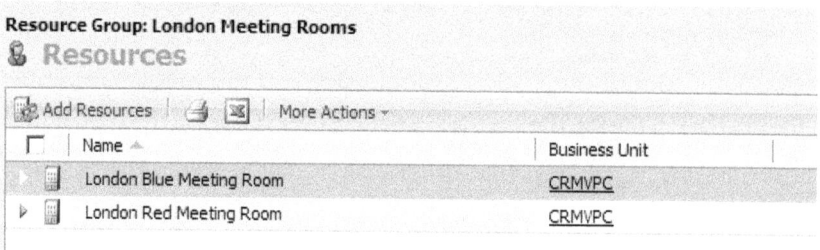

Taking advantage of the various options for configuring **service types** (see below) can satisfy simple scheduling requirements, such as allocating appointments at a dentist, as well as complex servicing activities requiring the booking of various items of equipment and engineers at different sites and taking into account the working hours for different shifts and the preferences of each customer.

14.2. Service Type

A **service type** must be defined in the **services-services** area (or in **settings-business management-services**) before a service activity can be scheduled.

The service type is used to define how long a service activity might take and the required resources so that the available time slots can be determined by the scheduling process. The **default duration** and **start activities** values determine the time slots available during the day and the **required resources** indicate which resources are required to perform each service activity.

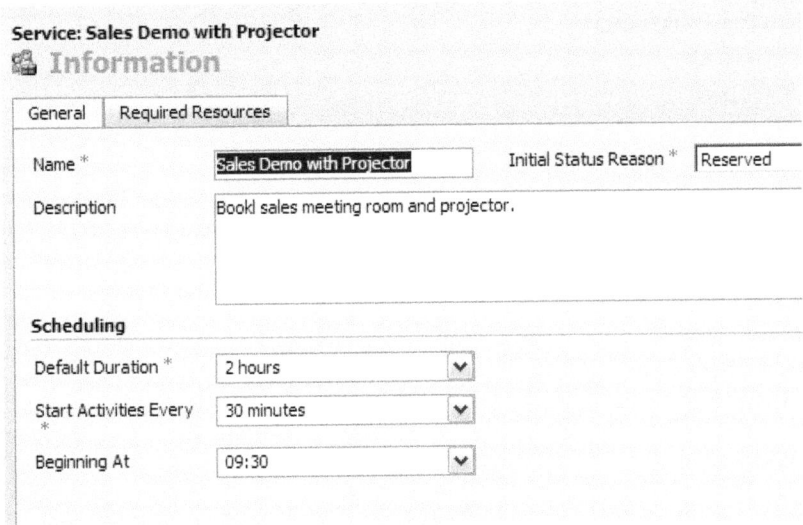

Each service type requires at least one resource which can be one of the following categories:

- **Facility/Equipment**.
- **User**.
- **Team**.
- **Resource Group**.

The **Required Resources** for a service can be quite sophisticated. This example is for a Sales Demonstration that requires all the following resources to be available at the **same site** for the Service Activity to be scheduled properly:

- A LCD Projector (equipment).
- A sales person chosen from the London Sales Team.
- A Meeting Room chosen from any of the rooms in the London Meeting Rooms Resource Group.

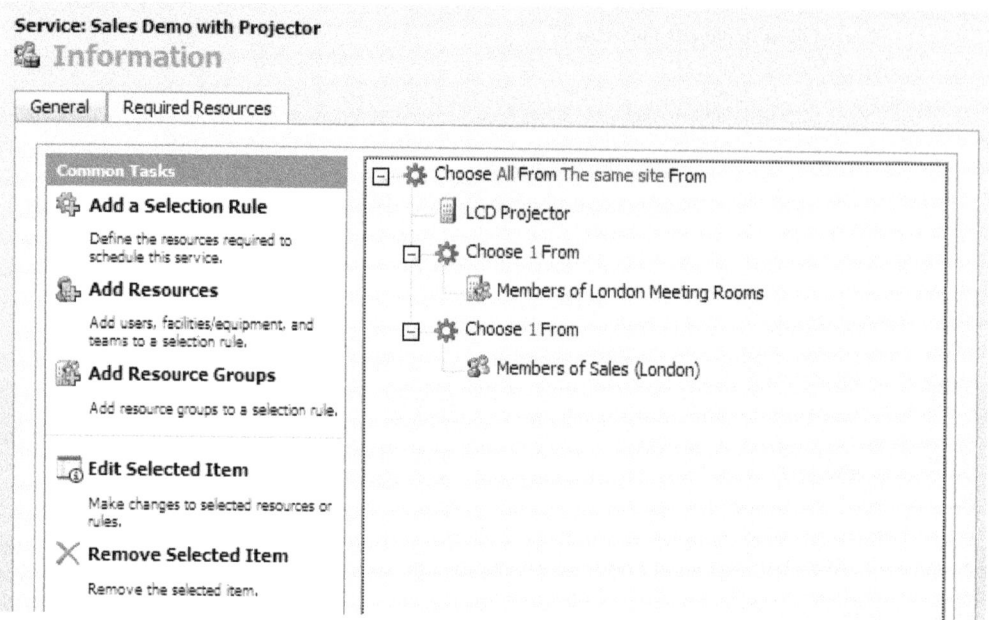

Resource Groups can be set up for interchangeable items in which case the **Choose 1 From** rule is selected. Alternatively a set of items can be combined and the **Choose All** rule specified so that all items in the group must be available to be scheduled for the service activity.

Double click on the wheel shaped icon of the selected resource to determine the **capacity** requirement (maybe you need two LCD projectors) and whether you want to choose the resource at **random** or select **the least or most busy** resource. The least busy option means that the least used meeting room is booked at any one time.

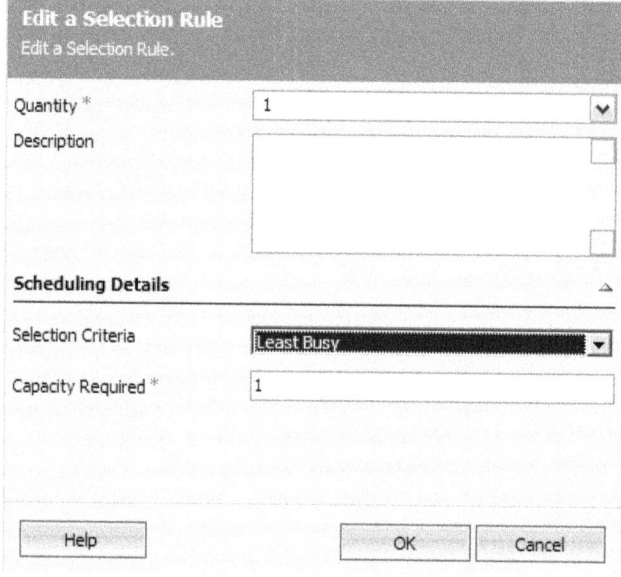

Note: The **more arrow** in the **scheduling details** section needs to be pressed to specify the selection criteria.

14.3. Scheduling an Activity

The creation of a Service Activity requires that a service type is selected to make the scheduling process available to help book a time when the required resources are available. Booked Service Activities appear in the **service calendar** and may be synchronised with Exchange and accessed from Outlook.

The **schedule** button shows the next free time at which all the resources required are available and allows them to be booked against the scheduled activity. The **service** and the **site** should be specified before the schedule button on the service activity form is pressed.

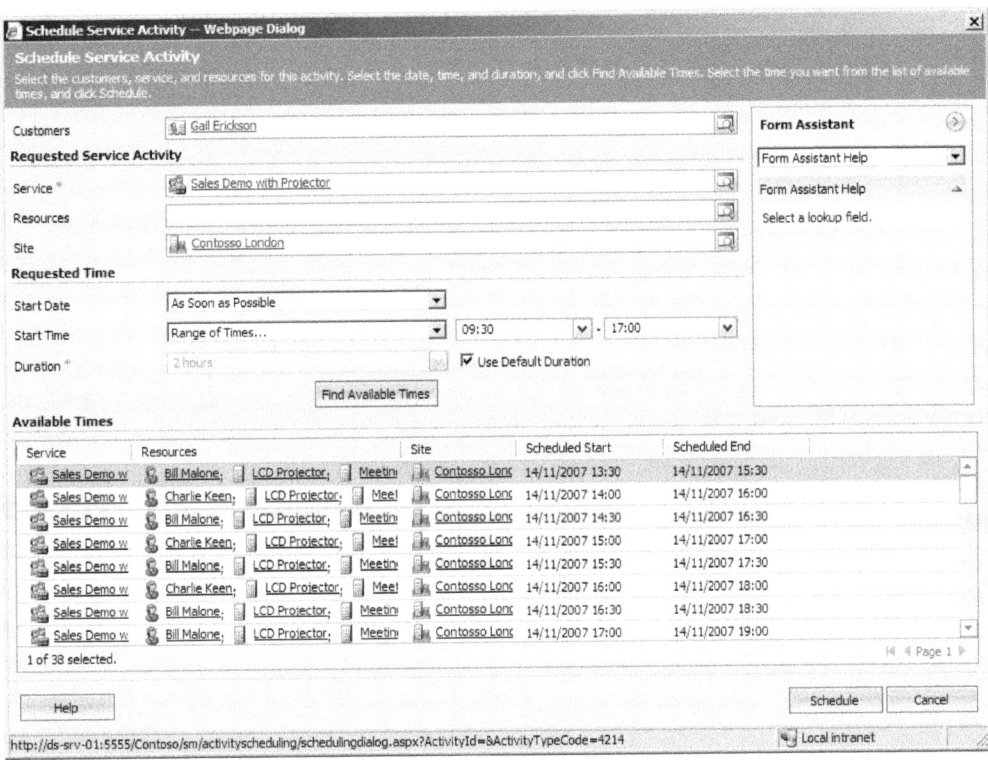

Select the required combination of resources and press the **Schedule** button to create the Service Activity record as required:

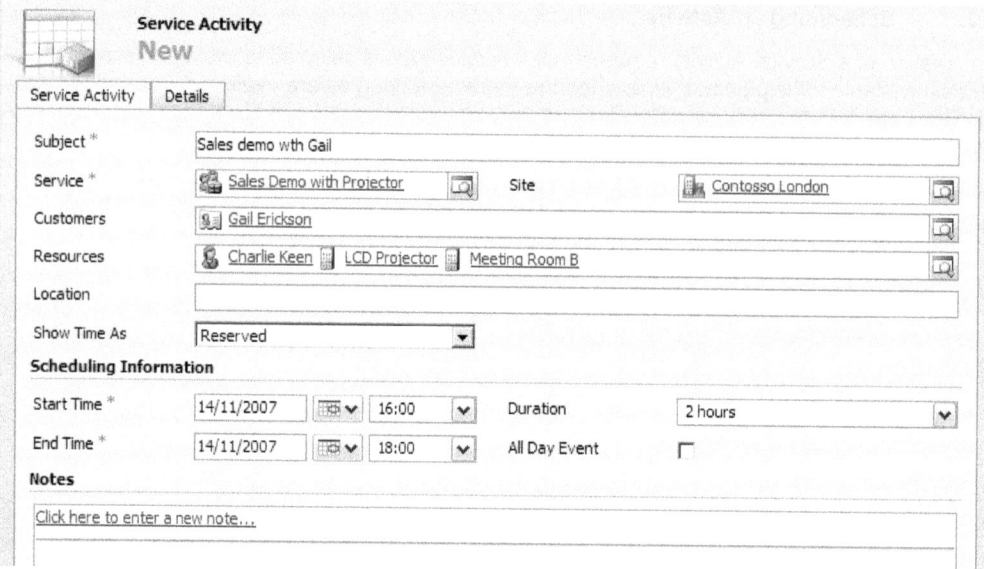

14.4. Preferred Resources

Preferred resources can be allocated to each customer so, for example, the regular service engineer that usually visits the customer can be the preferred engineer to book if available for a service call. This is available (by default) in the **administration** tab of the **customer form**.

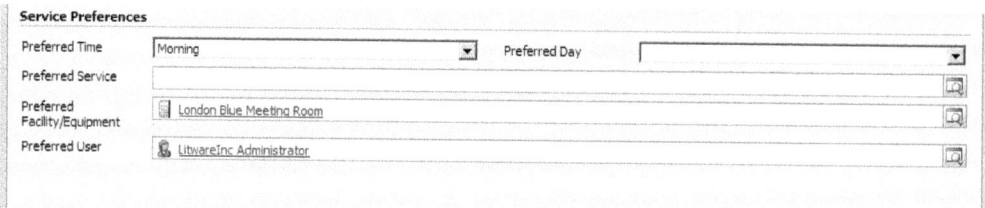

14.5. Service Calendar

The **service calendar** is more detailed than the **workplace calendar** which shows only information relating to the current user.

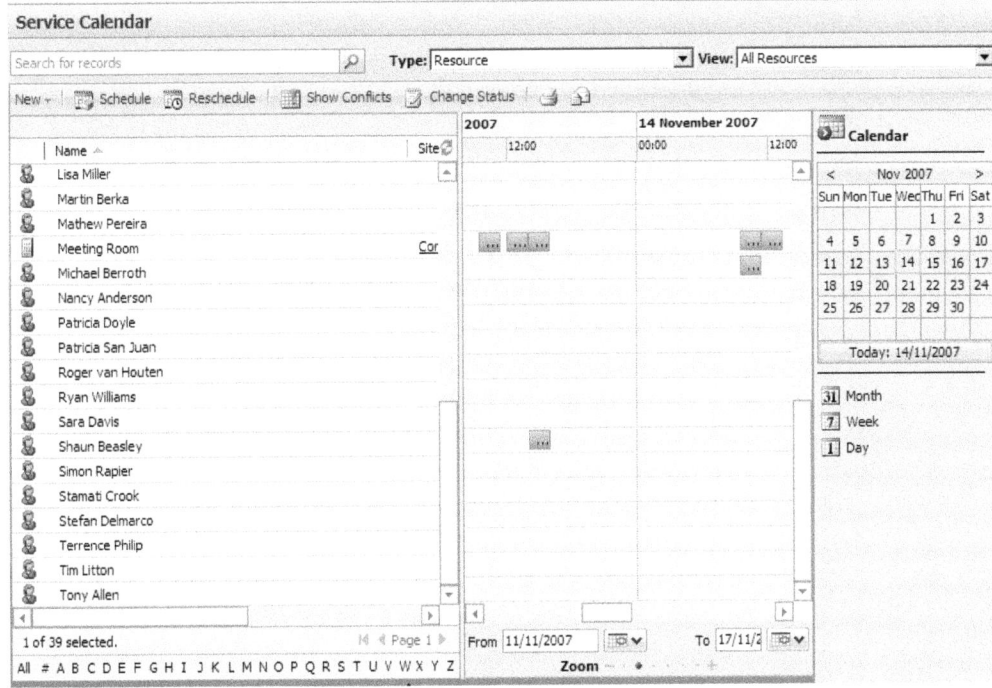

Views can be selected (and defined) to show a smaller number of relevant resources, and the calendar expanded or collapsed to show the required level of detail. Several advanced scheduling functions are available from the toolbar:

- New Service Activities can be created with the **schedule** button.
- Clicking on a service activity allows the **reschedule** button to suggest alternative dates (when all resources are available).
- **Show conflicts** helps the administrator resolve any double bookings.
- **Change status** changes the status of the service activity (for example from reserved to completed).

14.6. Business Closures

Business Closures allow public holidays and company closures to be specified and interact with the scheduling of resources.

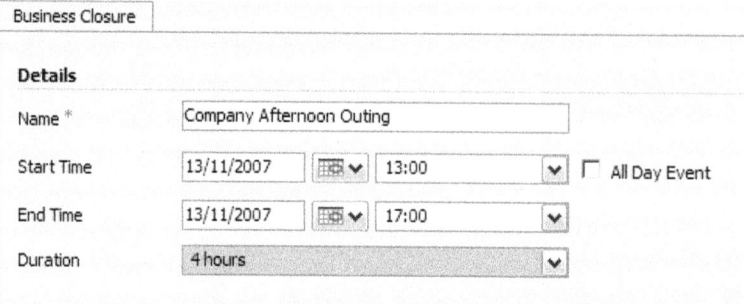

15. Reports

This chapter covers the use of the **report wizard** for creating reports that are integrated with CRM and output reports based on the records in the currently selected view (or form) to a variety of outputs including pdf and Excel.

Note: The report wizard actually creates a report file within SQL Server 2005 Reporting Services which can be worked on and extended by a developer if more complexity is required.

There are a number of alternative methods for extracting data from CRM which could be considered before creating a report:

- Personal **views** can be defined easily to export (and re-import) data from CRM using a spreadsheet.
- **Mail merge** files can be saved as a means of exporting address information.
- Complex **SQL Server reports** can be created by a programmer and integrated with CRM.
- The CRM **database** can be accessed directly (using **ODBC**) from an external program or reporting software (for example Crystal reports).

You should note that the CRM database is a SQL Server database and can be accessed directly using a variety of standard software, including Microsoft Access and Office, Crystal reports and many other report writers and database access software programs.

Note: Remember to log in to the database using your windows identity so that the CRM security settings are preserved and to use only the views prefixed with the word **filtered**.

15.1. Report Viewer

Reports can be integrated and run from several different places within the CRM interface:

- Reports can be called from the **workplace-reports** area with default or custom selection criteria.
- Reports can be run from the current **view**, which allows a single record or all records in the current view to be selected. The user can also **control+click** on a selection of required records to be included in the report.
- Reports can be called when looking at a **form** in which case just a single record is selected for the report.

Reports appear in a **report viewer** which may allow items to be **sorted** by clicking on the arrows to the right of the column heading (some reports also have drill down facilities and hyperlinks). The user can also print the report or choose a format for exporting to a file.

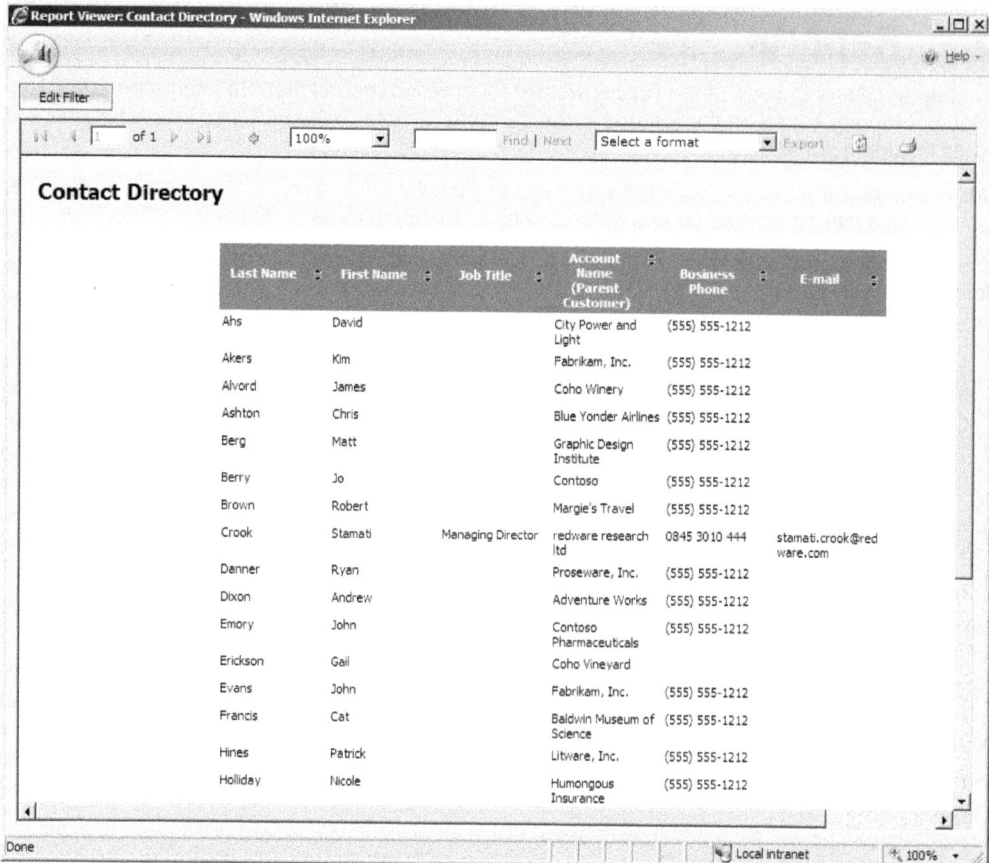

Reports can be exported into several different formats:

- **XML**. XML is a good format for exporting to other applications (and particularly good for programmatic access).
- **CSV**. CSV is a general format readable by the widest range of software programs.
- **TIFF**. This is an old graphic format and not recommended.
- **Adobe PDF**. PDF documents are the best format for distributing reports widely and can be printed from any machine (you need to download the free Adobe Reader).
- **Excel**. Reports is exported as a spreadsheet and formatting is preserved as much as possible. This is a good format for distributing to other users who need to cut and paste the data.
- **Web Archive**. A proprietary Microsoft format easily publishable as web pages accessible from a browser (not recommended).

Note: Selecting an output format requires the **export to excel** security permissions to be available to the current user.

15.2. Report Wizard

The **Report Wizard** allows the creation of simple reports (implemented in SQL Reporting Services) that are automatically integrated into CRM.

You can start the report wizard by creating a new report from the **workplace-reports** work area and you can modify an existing report or start from scratch. You need to specify a report **name** and choose the base **entity** (or **record type**) for the report. You can also choose a **related entity** here to show related records for the base entity (usually a one-to-many relationship, for example activities against a contact).

The next page allows you to specify report **filtering criteria.** Perhaps you can **clear** these and specify them in the reports form at the end of the process. Press **next** and the **Lay Out Fields** form appears, allowing you to add fields to the report and specify the **sorting criteria**.

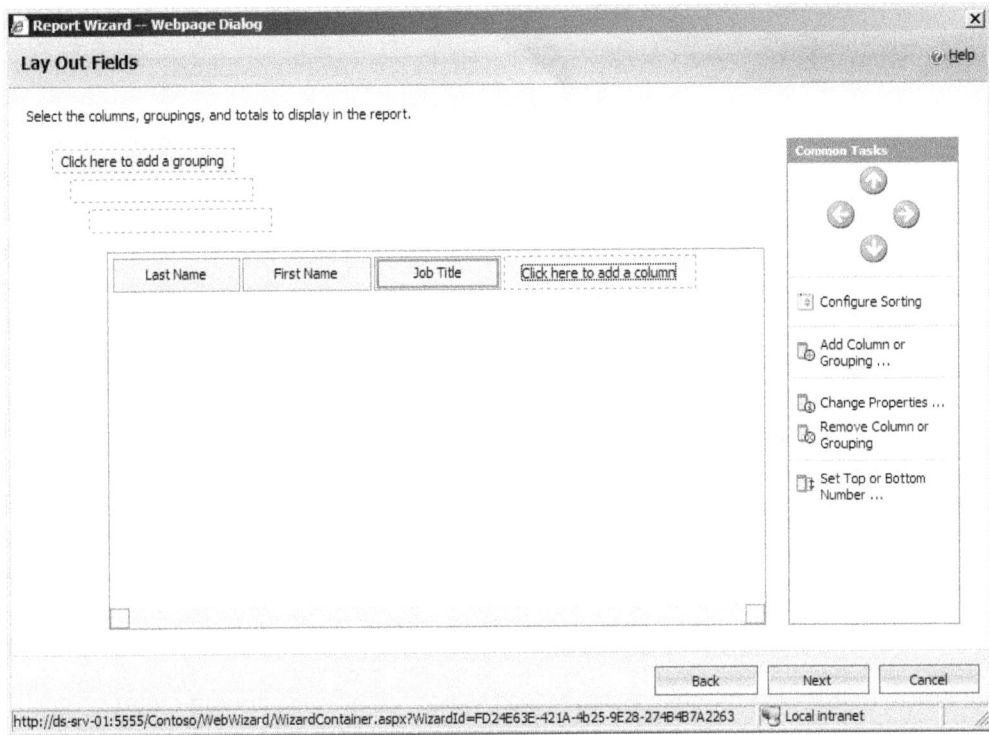

To add fields click on the **Click here to add a column** button and select the required field. You can select from the base entity and all related entities also (just many-to-one relationships) and can use the **Change Properties** button to change the width of the column. Use the green arrows to move the selected column and change the order of the columns in the report.

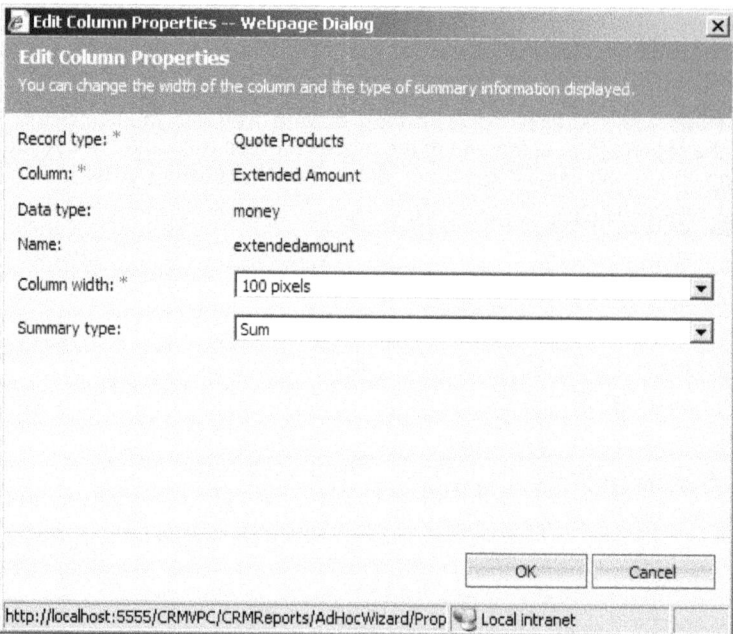

You can **add a group** to the report selecting the **click here to add a group** option and picking the appropriate field to group on. This allows you to specify **totals** for each numeric field and will be used if you want to create a chart in the report. Click on **Configure Sorting** to specify the default sort selection.

You will be prompted to add a **chart** to the report before finalising it. You can run the report wizard against the report at any time again to modify your report design.

The report form appears once the report has been completed and allows you to fine tune the integration with CRM. You can change these report settings by selecting the **edit-report** options from the actions menu in the **workplace-reports** area after you have selected the report in the report list.

	Report
	Contact Directory

General

Source

Report Type	Report Wizard Report
	Click Report Wizard to create or modify the report.
	[Report Wizard]

Details

Name *	Contact Directory
Description	Simple listing of basic contact details.

Parent Report

Parent Report	

Categorization

Categories	Administrative Reports;Marketing Reports;Sales Reports;Service Reports
Related Record Types	Contacts
Display In	Forms for related record types;Lists for related record types;Reports area
Languages	English

The **categories** section simply specifies the views within the **workspace-reports** work area which present the report. A more important integration feature is the **Display In** option, which provides the three kinds of integration mentioned earlier:

- **Forms**. This allows a report to run when viewing a single record in a form.
- **Lists**. Allows a selection of records from the current view to be included in the report.
- **Reports**. Adds the report to the **workplace-reports** work area according to the **categories** specified and uses the **default filter** to select records.

You should set the **default report filter** for each report (available from the actions menu of the report view) to select an appropriate range of records if you are calling the report from the workplace. The default filter can be overwritten when running the report and is not required for reports only called from a view or a form.

You can **share** your report with other users or make it available to the whole organisation from the actions menu on this form. A programmer can **download** the report to do further modifications and you can also **schedule** the report to run automatically within SQL Reporting Services or make it available to **external users**.

15.3. Running Reports

Reports can be run by pressing the **report** button available, where a report has been specified, on a form or a view.

Note: Running a report from a View allows individual records to be selected with **control+click**.

You have much more control over reports when running from the **workspace-reports** area. You can run or edit the report or run the report wizard again to change the report specification.

The **report filter** allows you to specify the filter selection on your report to produce summaries according to, for example, a date range or include only items created within the last month.

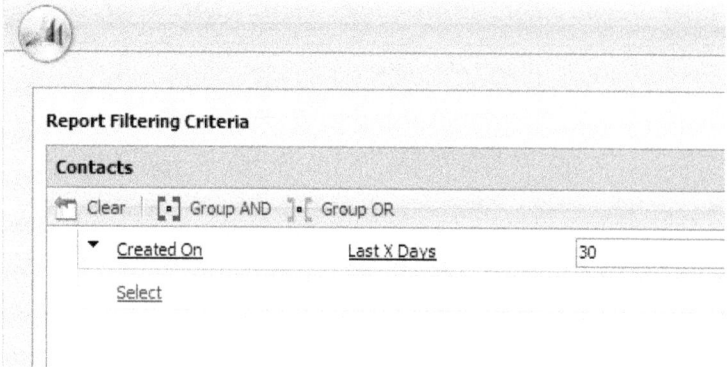

Quite complex report selection criteria, including related entities, can be built, and the filter criteria can be overwritten by the end user when running the report.

15.4. Scheduling Reports

Reports can be scheduled to run at particular times to save on resources when many different people want to view the same report. Select the scheduling option from the actions menu of the report selected in the **workplace-reports** area:

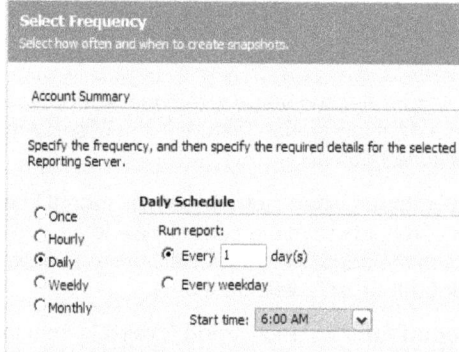

15.5. SQL Server Reporting Services

Microsoft CRM reports are built on top of a software technology known as **SQL Server Reporting Services**. Previous versions of CRM required technical expertise in this technology in order to build even simple reports which can now be built using the Report Wizard.

There are limitations to the complexity and power of reports created with the Report Wizard and all reports can be **downloaded** and worked on by a programmer and still remain integrated with CRM. More complex reports may need to be created from scratch by the programmer.

Note: Existing reports can be **downloaded** from the CRM environment (select a report in the **workplace-reports** area and use the action menu) and modified by a programmer using the report designer in **Visual Studio 2005**.

16. Workflow

Workflow is one of the key features that differentiates Microsoft CRM from other solutions. Microsoft regards workflow as so important that it has built a complete framework into the operating system. This means that workflow can be integrated with almost any application running on windows.

The **windows workflow foundation** allows programmers to create programs that stop and start and wait for something to happen just as a business process might do. For example, checking the credit status of an applicant for a mortgage may require many sequential or simultaneous tasks to be performed. Windows workflow allows such complex processes to be modelled in software.

Microsoft CRM 4.0 uses the new workflow engine but allows you to create your own workflow using the CRM application. Workflows operate automatically when certain things change on a record and they can be specified in the **settings-workflow** work area of CRM.

Note: *Workflow can be extended by a programmer using the Windows Workflow Foundation tools for Visual Studio 2005.*

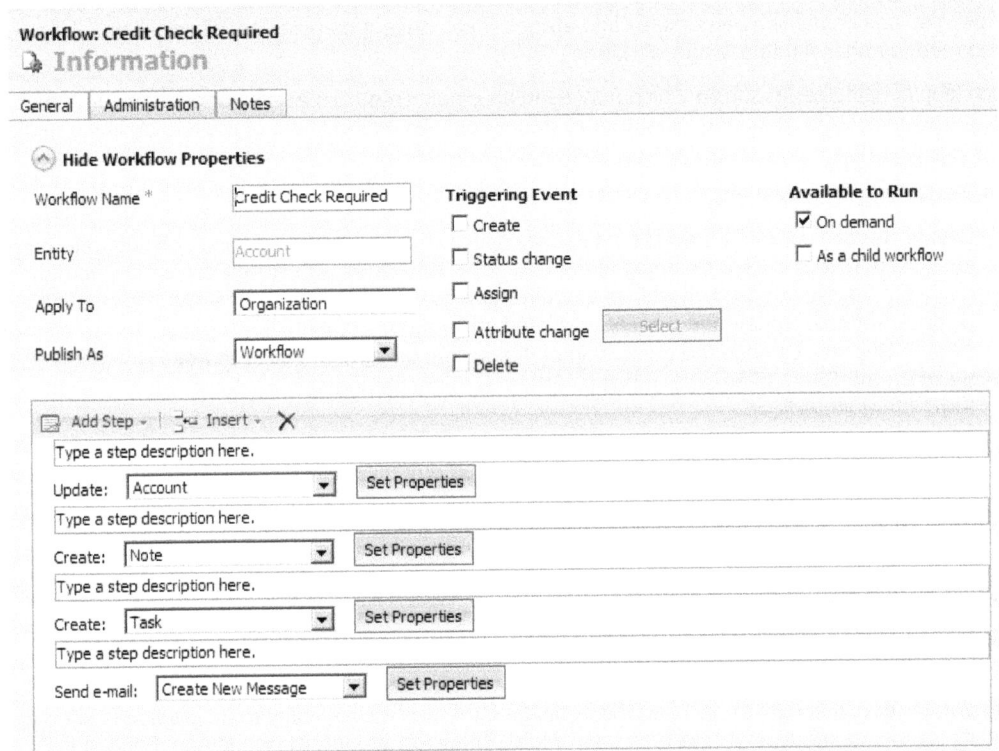

Each workflow is given a **name** and an **entity** to which it applies and it can **apply to** just the current user, their business unit or the whole organisation. This allows you to create workflow for just the sales department, for example. In addition, a workflow can be saved as a **template** to form the basis of other workflows.

16.1. Workflow Triggers

Workflows are triggered by an event happening within CRM, usually by a someone creating or altering data. The available triggers are:

- **Create**. The trigger fires automatically when a record is created (as the new record is saved).
- **Status Change**. The status values against an entity are easily customised and should reflect the relevant stage in the **life history** of the entity. A change in the status is a good place to create workflow actions which will vary according to each stage in the business process.
- **Assign**. Change of ownership (perhaps from a queue to a user) can automatically fire a workflow trigger.
- **Attribute Change**. Changes to particular field values in the database can automatically fire a trigger to start a business process. This could, for example, trigger a workflow when a custom checkbox is ticked.
- **Delete**. Automatic trigger to carry out a process when an entity occurrence is deleted.

Workflows can also be triggered **on demand** and are made available against the **activate workflow** button that appears on the actions menu when viewing a form.

Finally, a reusable **child workflow** can be specified which can be called from other workflows.

16.2. Workflow Steps

The lower half of the workflow pane contains the workflow process, which is specified as a series of **steps**. You can combine several steps into **stages** if you have a complex set of activities to be performed together within a single workflow.

Each step constitutes an **action** which may send an email, create an activity or change some data within the entity or related entity occurrences. More complex actions can, of course, be implemented by programmers.

The available action types are:

- **Create Record**. Create a new record usually specifying a related entity and defining data from the current record to give meaning to the new data. **Activities** and **Notes** can be created and related to the base record as well as any other entity.
- **Update Record**. Update the current or related entity data.
- **Assign Record**. Change the ownership of the current or related entity records.
- **Send Email**. Send an email or email template (with attachments).
- **Start Child Workflow**.
- **Change Status**. Changing the status of the current record is especially useful if you make the status field read-only so that it can only be changed automatically by workflow once all the relevant data has been specified and checked.
- **Stop Workflow**. Workflow is designed to pause and restart as the various processes are completed. This action indicates that the business process is complete.

16.3. Dynamic Values

The following screenshot shows the creation of a task activity during workflow triggered on the account entity.

The **create record** action is used and the template form for the task entity to be created is used to specify the values required for the new task record. The **form assistant** on the right hand side allows you to place **dynamic values** into the form. These values allow you to relate the newly created record to the current workflow entity occurrence.

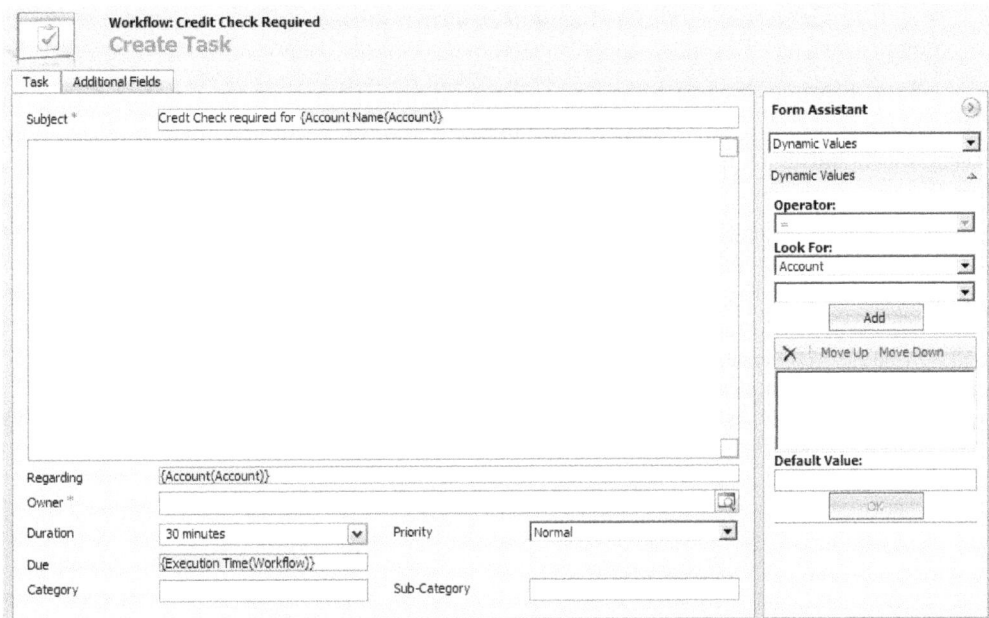

You can see in the example that the **regarding** value is set to the **account** entity and the **account name** is referenced in the subject field value. This is done by positioning the cursor in the required field on the form template and then selecting the required field in the dynamic values, pressing the **add** button and specifying any **default text** (to be entered if there is no value in the required field). Pressing **OK** will insert the appropriate dynamic value into the form.

Note: You can add more than one dynamic field value into the list of fields, and the first one in the list with a value will be inserted or the default value used if none of the fields have a value.

16.4. Workflow Conditions

Workflow conditions allow a single workflow to have a number of outcomes according to the state of the underlying data at the time the workflow is executed. The following example stops a workflow if a value has already been entered into the **credit limit** field of the account.

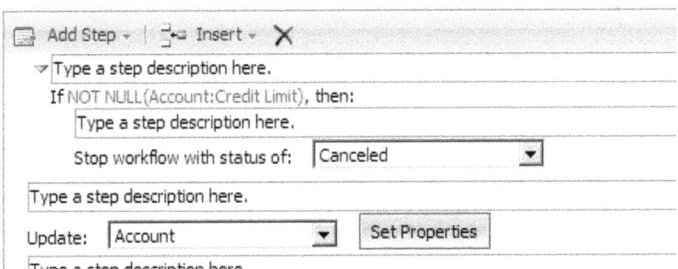

Conditions are very useful for the **change status** type of workflow to allow a single workflow to carry out different steps according to the current value of the entity status.

16.5. Wait Conditions

Wait conditions can be specified on workflow so that the workflow pauses and waits for a change to occur on the entity data before proceeding (this is a feature of the windows workflow framework).

Note: *This may be preferable to the alternative of creating a second workflow rule on the attribute change event.*

16.6. Sales Pipeline Phases

Workflow can be applied to most entities in CRM but workflow against **opportunities** can be used in conjunction with updating the **pipeline phase** and the **probability** values to help drive the **sales pipeline** reporting process.

The idea is to create a series of workflows against the opportunity entity to reflect the stages in the sales processes of the organisation. Each stage (or pipeline phase) may require a number of tasks to be carried out and successful completion leads on to the next stage in the pipeline. As each stage processes, the probability of a successful sale increases.

The workflow needs to be created against the **opportunity** entity and is available **on demand** in this case and can be activated once the opportunity has been created with the **run workflow** button on the opportunity form toolbar. This workflow is made available to everyone in the same **business unit** as the creator of the workflow.

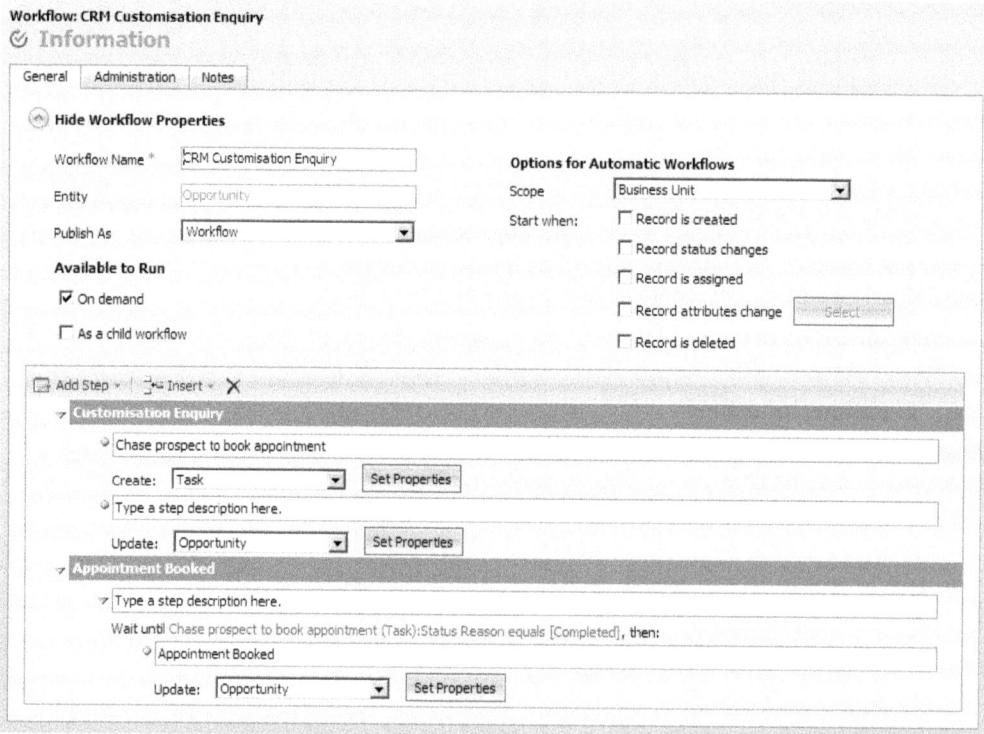

The **add step** button is used to add the first stage which refers to the Customisation Enquiry pipeline phase. The **insert action** is used to create a task that is due in three days time and prompts the owner to try and schedule an appointment.

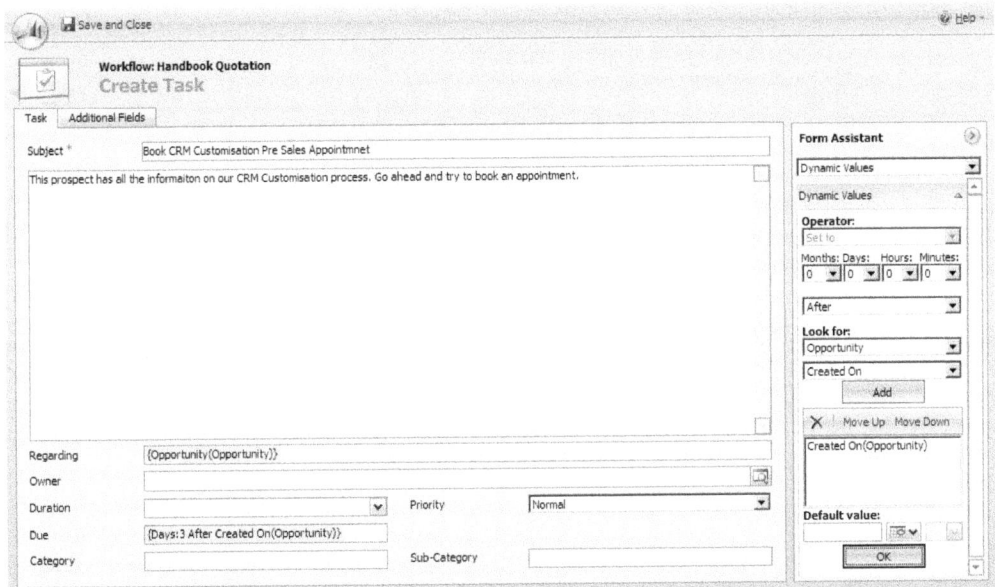

A second action is added to update the opportunity record and set the pipeline phase to have the value **Customisation Enquiry** and the probability to 5.

A second stage is added which has a wait condition that waits for the task created in the first phase to be completed and then changes the pipeline phase to **Appointment Booked** and the probability to 15%.

Once you have created the opportunity, the workflow can be run from the run workflow button and automatically sets the pipeline phase to Customisation Enquiry, the probability to 5% and creates the task against the opportunity. You may need to wait a little **or press f5 to refresh** the form for the workflow to appear in the **workflow area** of the navigation pane.

The workflow process shows which stages in the workflow process have been completed.

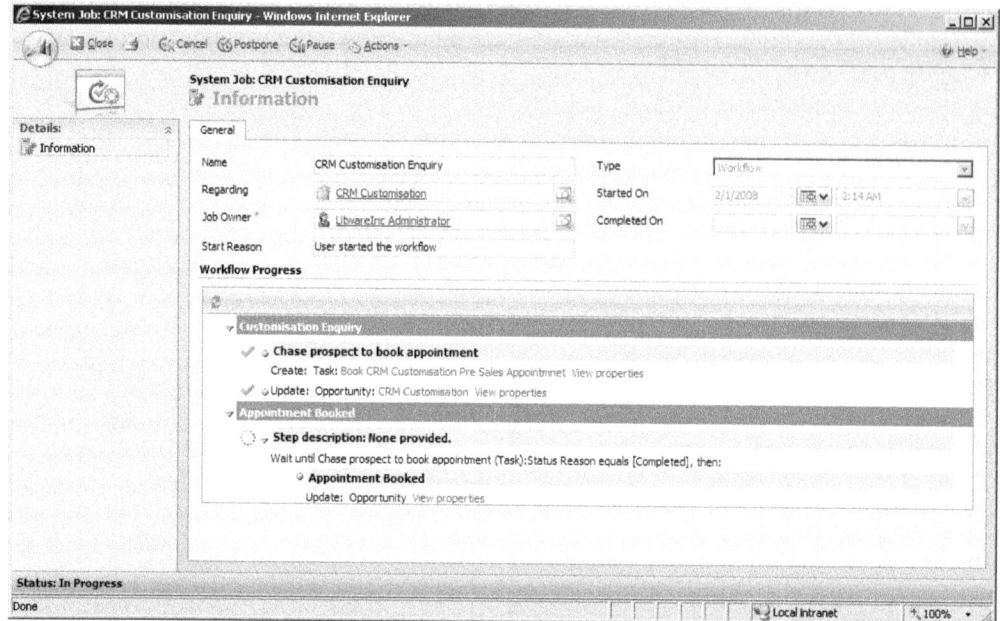

Completing the task will move the pipeline phase on to the next stage setting the probability to 15%.

17. Security

CRM has sophisticated security configuration facilities that use a combination of **business units** and security **roles** to determine the information and functionality available to each user within CRM.

Each record in CRM (except for organisation-owned entities) is assigned an **owner** who belongs to a **business unit**. It is the business unit that determines the security and each user is given a number of roles that determine whether they can access just records they own or access all the records belonging to the same business unit or those lower down in the hierarchy.

The following concepts apply to CRM security:

- **Root Organisation** – the root business unit for the installation.
- **Business Unit** – a hierarchical structure reflecting the organisation of the business, perhaps according to business function (sales, marketing, customer service) for a smaller company. Each user belongs to one business unit.
- **User** – a user is assigned to a single business unit and has one or more security roles. The least restrictive security setting against all of the roles assigned to a user determines the security level.
- **Roles** – the security role determines the security permissions available against each entity or function. Roles are defined against the root organisation or for a particular business unit and are inherited by the child business units.
- **Teams** – individual records may be shared with individual users or with teams of users. Although teams have a default business unit, any user can be assigned to a team.

Teams allow for exceptions to be made to the security depending on the business unit hierarchy and individual records can be shared with any individual user or team.

The Enterprise version of CRM offers **multi-tenancy** where multiple instances of the CRM database can run side by side on the same hardware with users being able to log in to each instance with a single user licence. This may be useful for larger companies where different divisions run entirely separate business processes which can be installed as independent databases.

17.1. Business Unit

An organogram of your organisation can be used to determine a hierarchy of business units (departments) within the organisation that is broken down so that all staff within each unit are likely to be sharing information with each other. Members of each unit can be assigned different security roles so that the manager role, for example, can view all information owned by a business unit but ordinary members can view only their own data.

Each business unit is part of a hierarchy (the parent business unit can be changed in the actions menu) and inherits the available security roles from its parent. It is recommended that security roles are maintained against the primary business unit so that each role has a similar definition throughout the organisation.

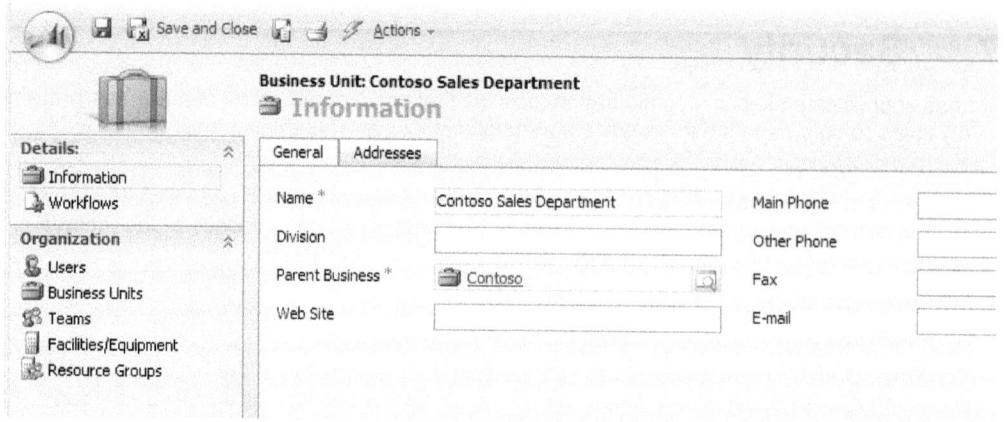

Security settings can be set up for each entity to **cascade** down to related (one to many) entities so that all related records have their ownership changed or are shared with a team when the parent record is assigned to another owner or shared (see the customisation section).

Business units can refer to external organisations that require access to CRM, such as resellers, affiliates or suppliers. Security can be set up so that these users can view and update data only within their own business unit. They can be made part of a team to be given access to other records only if the record is shared with the appropriate team.

Note: *Take care when setting up the business units as the names cannot be changed after they have been entered.*

17.2. Users

All user settings can be configured within the **settings-business units** option, and new users can also be created and altered here. Note that new users must first be created in the Windows Active Directory and that deleting or changing the user details within Active Directory does not automatically update the entry in CRM.

Entering the Domain Logon Name for a new user will automatically extract the remaining details from the Active Directory.

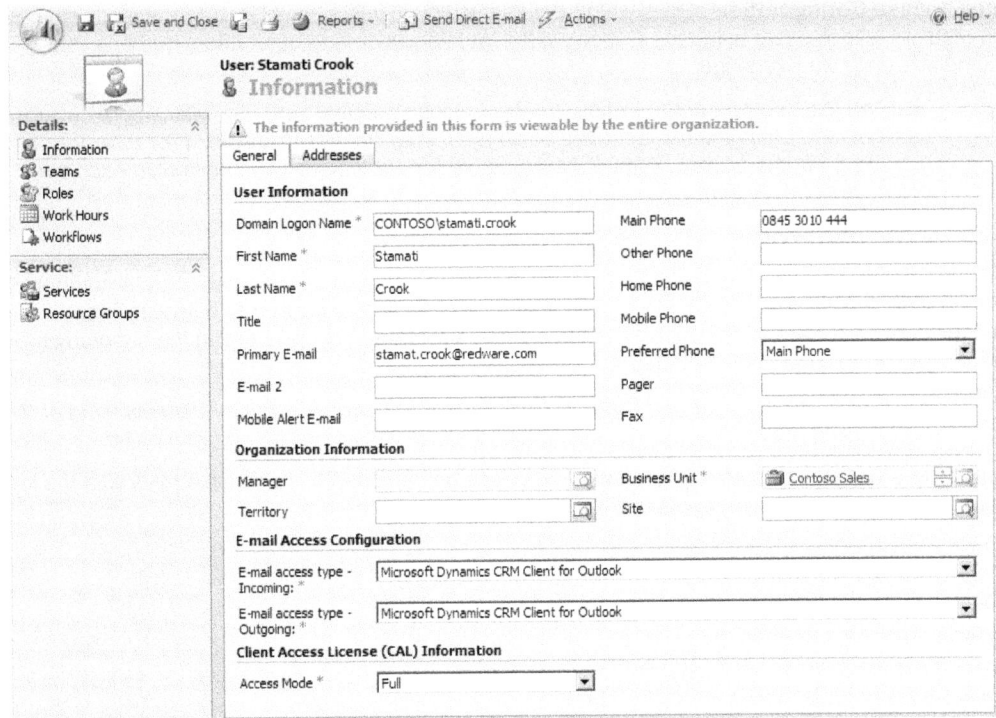

The **Organisation Information** for a User is useful in different areas of the application:

- **Manager** can be used to create workflow and for reporting analysis.
- **Business unit** is the core organising principle behind the ownership of data and security.
- **Territory** is used for assigning leads and monitoring the sales cycle.
- **Site** is used to determine location for scheduling.

Note: Multiple users can be entered from the **new-add users** option.

Changing the business unit for a user will affect the security settings on all of the records owned by the user and needs some care. All of the owned records can be reassigned before changing the business unit with the **reassign records** option on the actions menu of the user form (you can also use the **assign** button available on the view toolbar).

The **manager** and **business unit** can be changed from the actions menu. Changing a business unit against a user deletes all of the roles, and the user will have no security rights to access the system until a new set of roles has been specified.

Users can be **enabled** and **disabled** and the number of full and read-only users should match the purchased licences. There are three different **access modes** for a user:

- **Full** provides access to the database according to the least restrictive of the assigned security roles.
- **Administrative** users have no access to data but can log on to the system and change settings (no licence required).
- **Read-only** users pay a reduced licence fee but cannot write to the database.

Note: Read-only and administrative users can be owners of tasks even though they cannot alter data, and workflow could be defined to carry out email notifications as necessary.

Email Access Configuration allows you to define the way in which email is synchronised with CRM with regular Outlook users using the Outlook client for integration and other users perhaps using automatic routing via Exchange.

Note: You can test different users without having to logon multiple times by selecting the **Internet Options** and changing the **Security** settings for your browser to **prompt for user logon** (usually for trusted sites). You will be prompted for a username and password each time you access the system.

17.3. Security Roles

Security settings for each role are defined for each entity or against specific functions. A number of default roles are set up during CRM installation and can be used or **copied** to help with initial configuration. Take care to create roles at the highest applicable business unit in the hierarchy so that changes are passed down throughout the system.

Note: **System Administrator** and **System Customiser** are special roles for administering and customising the system.

Remember also that users belong to a single business unit and can have multiple roles with the least restrictive security permission applied where appropriate.

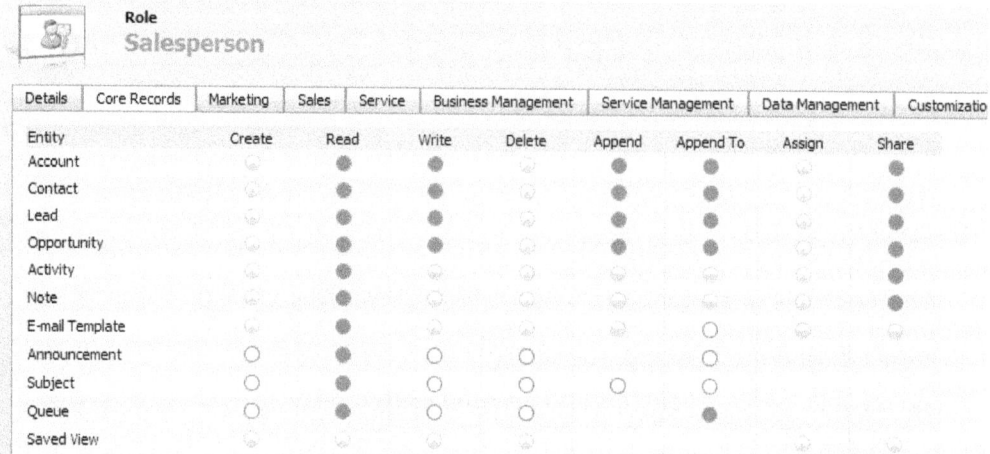

Security settings can be established at the following levels:

- **None** – no access permitted.
- **User** – the user can access entity occurrences that he or she owns, along with entities that have been shared explicitly with that user or a team to which the user belongs.
- **Business Unit** – the user can access any entity owned by members of their business unit.
- **Child Business Unit** – the user can access any entity owner by their business unit or any business unit lower down in the hierarchy.
- **Organisation** – access to everything.

Most entities have **user-based ownership**, and the owning business unit is determined by the owner of the record. Changing the owner, using the **assign** button, may in some cases also change the business unit affecting the access rights on that entity occurrence. Changing the business unit for a user will also change the Business Unit of all of the entity occurrences owned by that User.

17.4. Teams

Teams are used to allow exceptions to the security levels. Perhaps some contacts need to be **shared** with users in separate business units, but the current security access level denies access. In this case, the entity occurrence can be shared with individual users or teams who then have the permitted access to that entity.

Note: *Teams are assigned to a default business unit, but this is just to limit the teams visible to other users. Any user can be specified as a member of any team.*

One problem with security is that the business unit is automatically assigned to each record according to the current owner and it does not seem possible to change this without reassigning the owner. This can cause problems when a department is sub-divided into several business units and the manager and administrative staff are in the parent business unit. In this case, any records created by the manager cannot be viewed by the users in the child business units and will have to be shared with a team.

18. Customisation

Microsoft CRM has a very robust software framework which enables end users to create and alter the database definition from the user interface. Technical skills are not required but permissions to perform customisation are usually reserved for the systems analyst or a **system customiser** who is in charge of making changes to the system.

This chapter discusses mainly entity customisation where existing and new entities can be defined in several ways:

- **Views** can be created for all users (personal views can also be shared by the user).
- Custom **entities** can be created.
- Existing entities can be modified and **attributes** (fields) changed or new fields added.
- **Forms** can be altered (only one form per entity).
- **Relationships** and **mappings** can be defined between entities (mappings automatically copy field values over from the parent when creating a child record).
- **Relationship roles** can be defined between the account, contact and opportunity entities.

Any changes made in this area are not reflected in CRM until the appropriate entity has been selected and the changes published by pressing the **Publish** button at the top of the page.

Before you add any new entities or attributes you should alter the **prefix** in the **customization** tab available from **settings-administration-system settings** to a unique prefix for your organisation. This ensures that your customisations cannot conflict with customisations that you may add later copied from another organisation or created by a software supplier.

18.1. Views

Views are very easy to change, and the users themselves can create their own views. A fully customised version of CRM may need many views changed, and this can take some time when you take into account the time spent liaising with the users.

There are several kinds of view:

- The **default** view (specified with the Actions menu) which is the view first seen when selecting on the entity.
- The **associated** view is seen when clicking on the navigation pane for a related (one-to-many) entity in a form.
- The **lookup** view is seen when looking up a related entity.
- **Quick find** views are used when searching in a View. Fields can be added to **find columns** in this view and used in the search.
- **Public** views are defined for all users.

Note: Personal Views can also be shared with other users by the owner.

Views can be edited (only if you have security rights), and you can add fields from any related (many to one) entity. The position of the fields can be changed by selecting the field and clicking the **green arrows**, and the field widths can be set with **change properties**.

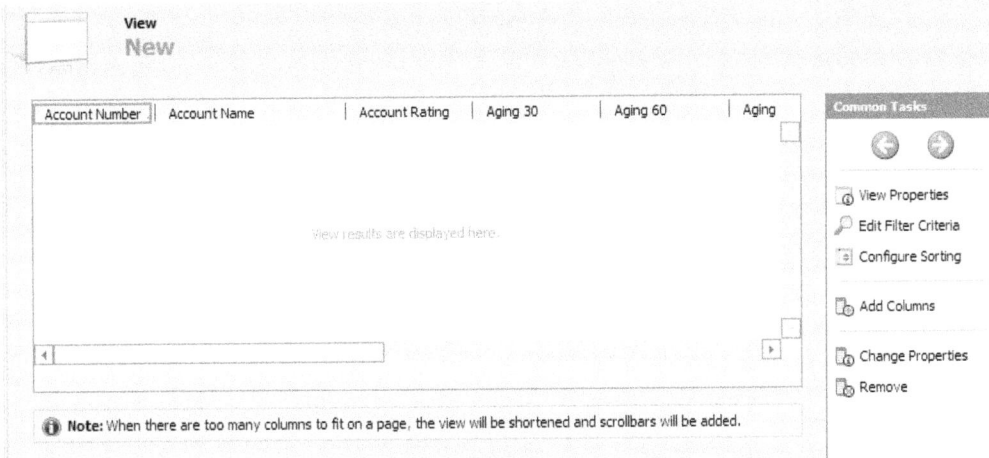

Each View can be **sorted** on any (single) field which also powers the alphabet bar along the bottom of the view to help selection. You might want to provide a view sorted by postcode or account number if users are constantly searching with these criteria.

The **filter criteria** can be specified so that only selected records are shown. The relationship type on the account entity might be used, for example, to select only customers in a View.

Note: Quick find views allow one or more **find columns** to be specified and are used to search through the table when using the search option for a view.

18.2.   Preview Form

The preview form is defined together with the views when customising an entity and allows for a collection of fields to be seen by toggling the **see more** triangle on the view without needing to launch the entity form.

18.3.   Entities

Existing entities can be extended or new entities defined.

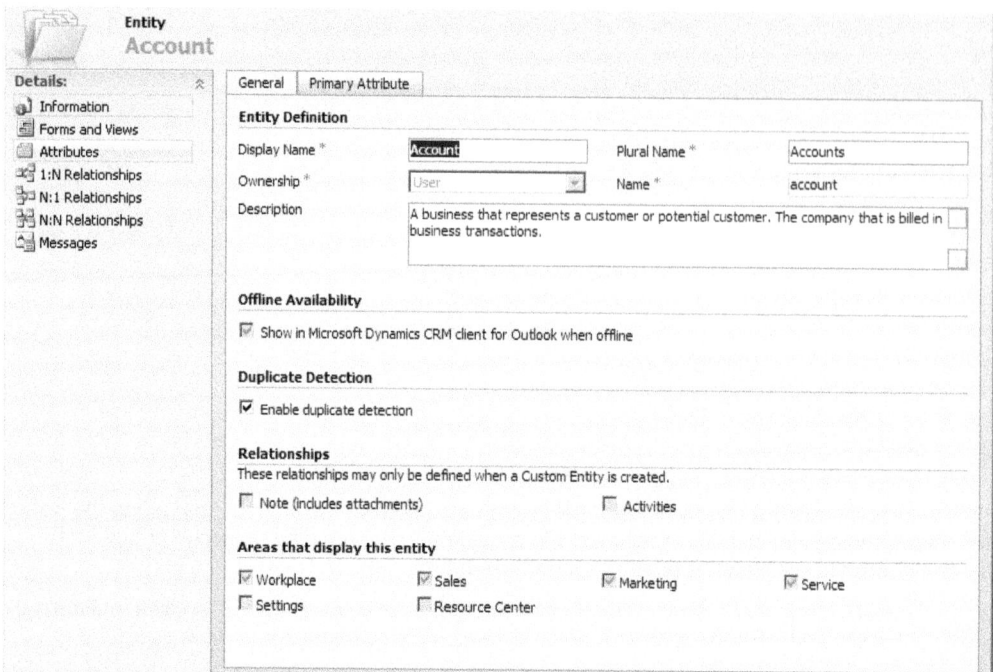

A new entity requires the following definitions, and take care, because some of these options cannot be changed once the entity has been created:

- **Name**.
- **Plural Name**.
- The **Primary Attribute** is used to describe the entity occurrence and is displayed as a hyperlink on a form where a relationship is made to the entity (take care as it cannot be changed later).
- **Organisation** or **User Ownership**. This affects security, as only user-owned entities can have business units and allow security to be defined.
- **Synchronisation with the Outlook Client**.
- Allow **Notes** or **Activities** to be added against the entity.
- The **Work areas** which display the entity can be specified.

Note: All new entities and attributes are automatically created with a **new_** prefix. It is a good idea to change this prefix in the Settings menu to a different value so that your customisations will not clash with other customisations that use the same prefix.

18.4. Attributes

Once an entity has been created, the **attributes** (fields) can be defined. Each field has a type and a **display name** and a **schema name**. The schema name and type are set into the database structure and cannot be changed once the attribute has been created.

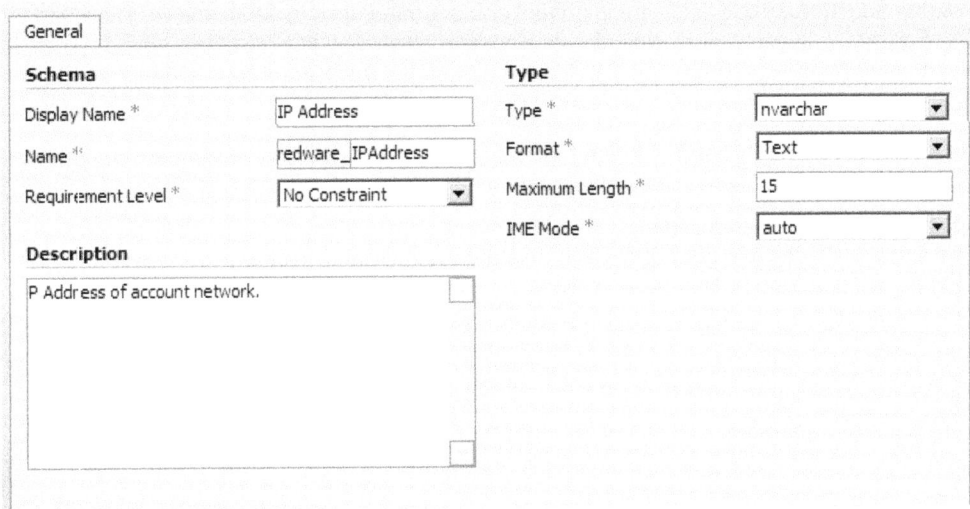

The **requirement level** is used to **recommend** or **require** that the value is entered by the user on a form. See the next section on how to edit the form to include the new field.

The following field types are available:

- **nvarchar** – Unicode text value formatted as text, an email address or URL, text area or ticker.
- **picklist** – integer representing a value defined in a list of options.
- **bit** – yes/no value
- **int** – an integer whole number formatted as an integer, a duration, or a time zone.
- **float** – a decimal number.
- **money** – a decimal number representing a currency value (which automatically stores both the currency and base currency values).
- **ntext** – a large piece of text such as a note (or email body).
- **datetime** – a datetime value which can be formatted to show just the date if required.

Selecting a type will change the available **format** options available.

Note: *Try to ensure that you always add and delete values together on all similar picklists, as CRM does not recognise the text value of the picklist when performing any mappings and always takes the integer value for comparison.*

You can view the entities and their definitions with a CRM utility page as follows (substitute your own server name into the URL):

http://crmserver:5555/sdk/list.aspx

http://crmserver:5555/sdk/mdbrowser/entity.aspx?entity=entityname

There are some system fields that are automatically defined for all entities:

- Primary Key (a GUID).
- Status.
- State.
- Owner.
- Relationships (many-to-one) have the primary attribute values as well as the foreign key identifier stored.
- Created and Modification dates.

The **status** and **statuscode** fields are important and are often used to define the workflow and the status of an entity on completion. Note that most related fields and picklist values store both the key value and a name value corresponding to a text value for the entity to make reporting easier.

18.5. Forms

Forms can easily be customised in a web-based editor available in the **settings-customizations-customize entities** work area. Each form is composed of several elements:

- **Tabs** across the top of the form.
- Each tab is divided into **sections** which may optionally display header information.
- **Fields** are positioned within each section.
- An **iframe** allows a URL to be specified to pull in information from an external website.

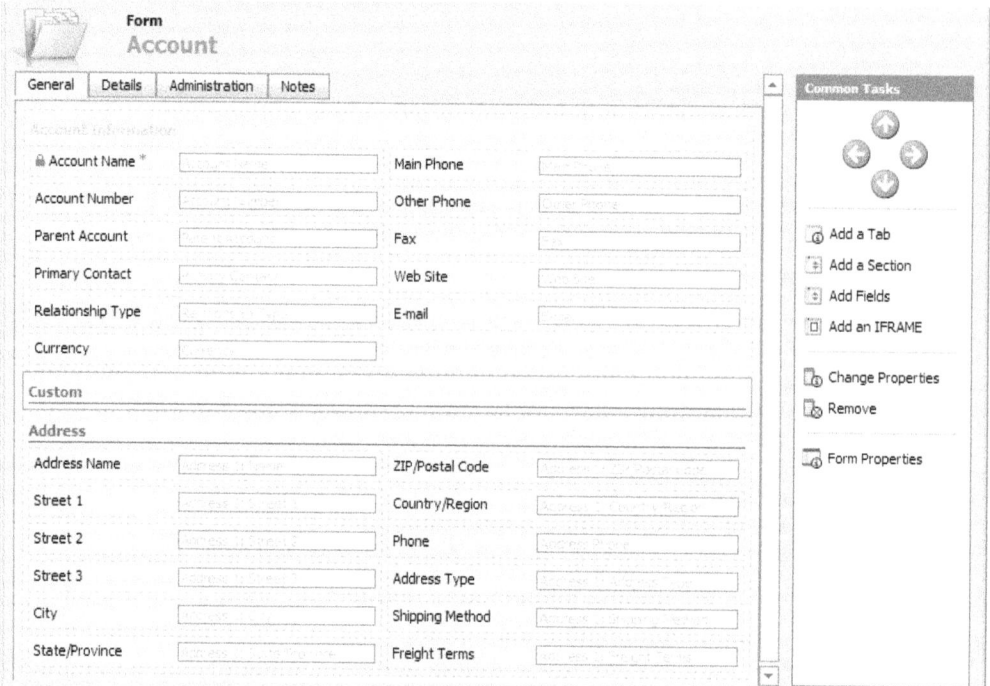

Fields can be moved around within a section with the green arrow buttons. Selecting the **change properties** option allows fields to be moved between sections and the **label** changed or the field **disabled** (made read-only). Removing a field removes it from the form only and not the database.

Note: *Security is applied to the whole record according to the business unit of the owner. Security on individual fields or tabs on the form must be implemented programmatically with JavaScript if different security is required for different users.*

18.6. JavaScript

The behaviour of a form can be modified with JavaScript to enable and disable fields and perform many other tasks.

CRM forms have a standard layout and functionality and programming with JavaScript allows you to customise the validations on fields and general behaviour to suit your exact requirements. Security is defined at record level and consequently JavaScript is used to disable fields according to user level security.

There are various JavaScript functions available within a CRM form to set field values, check the status of the form (is it being run from a laptop, for example), save the form and so on. Examples can be found online, and we recommend that programmers read the **Working with CRM** book for more information (see the resources section).

Note: The use of Ajax programming techniques can make JavaScript programming a very powerful feature.

The form designer allows JavaScript code to be pasted into **form level** and **field-level events** and the **preview** button allows some limited testing to take place before publishing the modified form.

There are two form-level events which can be customised with JavaScript code:

- **OnLoad** – this allows the form to be initialised as it is loaded.
- **OnSave** – form level validation occurs here with a false value returned to prevent the form from updating.

Field level events comprise just the **OnChange** event which fires each time the field is updated. The example below shows how a programmer can add an onchange event to the quantity field on a quotation and automatically calculate the tax.

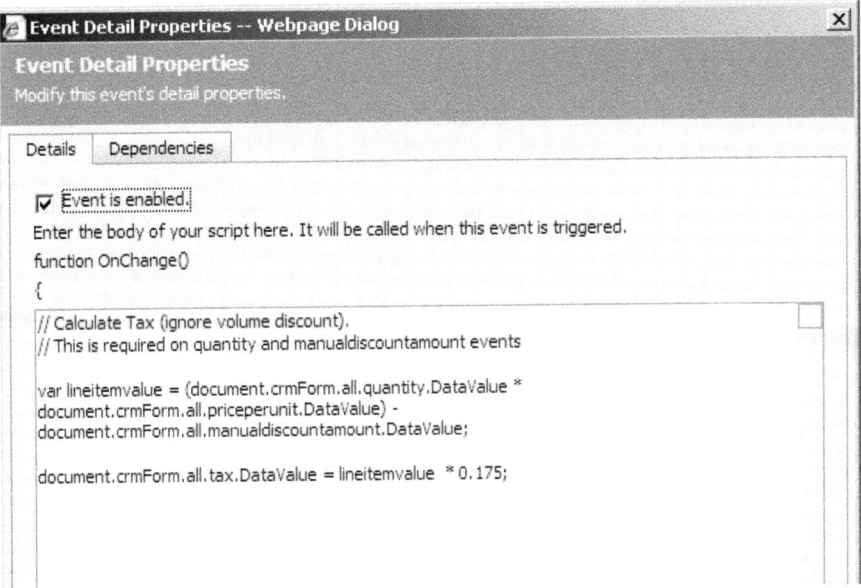

Note: Programmers can also access the internal functionality of CRM with plug-ins and you might want to disable the tax field and calculate it automatically as the data is saved.

18.7. Iframes

IFRAMES allow integration with external websites and help programmers to integrate with CRM by displaying related web pages such as a map related to the address. Most of these integrations will require some JavaScript or the passing of the object level identifiers to the page.

18.8. Relationships

Custom entities usually require that one or more **relationships** are defined to relate the entity to existing entities already in CRM. Relationships can be of several types:

- **1:N** or one-to-many. For example, each order may have many order items.

- **N:1** or many-to-one. For example, each order item belongs to just one order.
- **N:N** or many-to-many relationship. For example, an account can have many contacts and each contact can be associated with several accounts.

Many-to-one relationships are important as they determine the entities which can be joined together easily to make fields available in a view. Each contact has a primary account so the two entities can be joined and fields from the primary account record displayed alongside the contact record. Fields from other related accounts (one-to-many or many-to-many) cannot be displayed in a view because the system cannot determine which of the many account records to display.

Note: Relationships can be self-referential so that a manager, for example, can be defined for contact records that refer to the manager also stored in the contact table.

The following screenshot illustrates the creation of a many-to-one relationship from a custom entity called **holiday** to the contact **entity**. The primary entity (contact) is the **one** side of the relationship, and the related entity (holiday) the **many** side so that each Contact can have many Holiday records but each Holiday just one Contact.

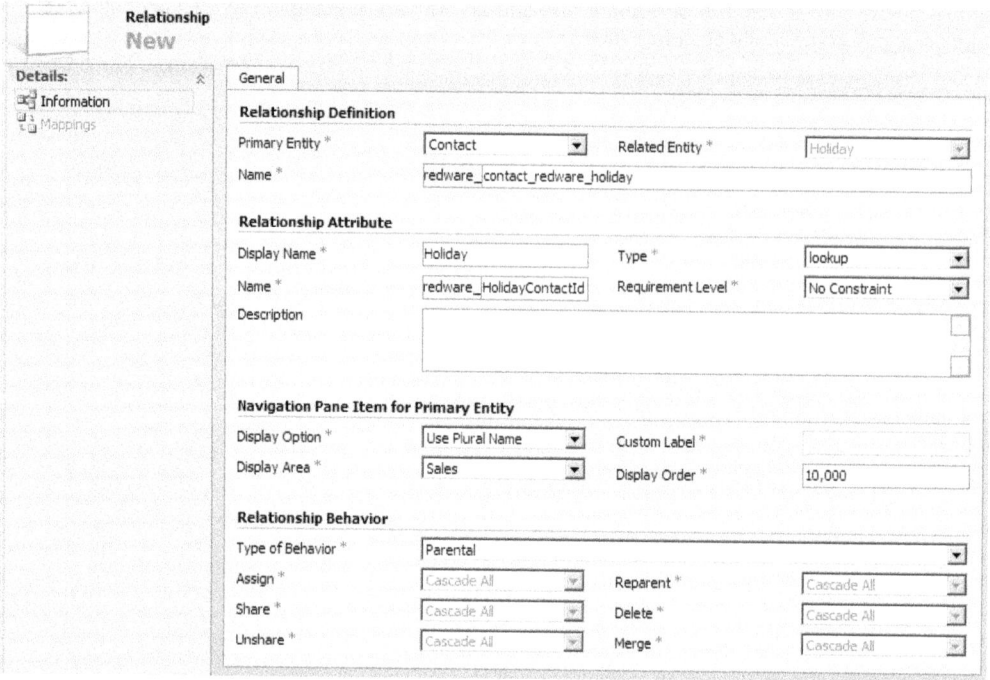

Publishing the customisations (for both contact and holiday) adds a new option into the **navigation pane** of the contact entity form showing Holidays. Selecting this pane allows new holidays to be added and related to the contact.

The Holiday entity is also made available from the sales work area, and adding a new Holiday record allows the user to look the Contact up to join the two records together. In this case, a Holiday record cannot exist without a related contact record in this example because of the **parental** relationship. Complex behaviour can be defined so that all holiday records are deleted, for example, if the parent contact record is deleted.

The available modes are:

- **Referential**. The many records can exist independently of the one record.

- **Parental**. The many records cannot exist independently of the one record.
- **Referential, Restrict Delete**. The one record cannot be deleted until all of the many records have been deleted.
- **Configurable Cascade**. Configure each feature manually so that changes in ownership and so forth cascade down from the one entity to the many records.

The cascading option extends past that of the behaviour of the Delete operation. The cascading options control the way in which the related records in a many-to-one relationship change if the parent record also changes. Changes to the Owner assigned to the master record, or to the Teams shared, can be passed on down to the related records.

Note: You may need to change some of the system relationship cascade behaviour to stop changes in the ownership of a Lead, for example, from reassigning all related activities to the new Owner.

The **Mappings** for a relationship allow fields to be copied automatically (from the one to the many entity) when a new entity is created. For example, the email address of the Contact is copied over automatically when the Holiday record is created from the contact form.

18.9. Renaming an Entity Description

An entity description can be changed, and CRM customisers often rename the Accounts entity as Company. You can easily rename the entity, but doing the job properly requires more than just changes to the entity name:

- Change the entity name and plural name.
- Rename any views.
- Rename any labels on the forms.
- Change system messages.
- Change labels in reports.
- Change the online help.

18.10. Relationship Roles

Relationship Roles can be defined between the core account, contact, and opportunity entities to capture relationships between entities. For example, you may sell services to doctors and their patients and need to keep track of their relationships.

In this case you might create a relationship called **doctor** to make relationships between the Doctor's Surgery (account) and their patients (contacts). This is an **account role for contacts** and you would also create the opposite **patient** relationship as a **contact role for accounts**.

The example below shows the creation by the system customiser of a relationship that operates between accounts and contacts:

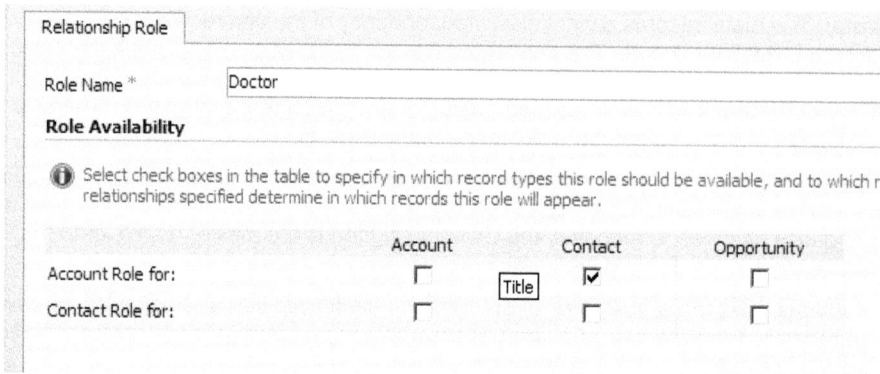

You can create the relationship from the contact (or the account) form by adding a new relationship from the **relationships** pane. Select the current contact record as **party 1** and then select the appropriate account record for the Doctor's surgery in **party 2**. Now you can specify the appropriate roles and use them later for marketing or informational purposes when communicating with the Doctor or their Patient.

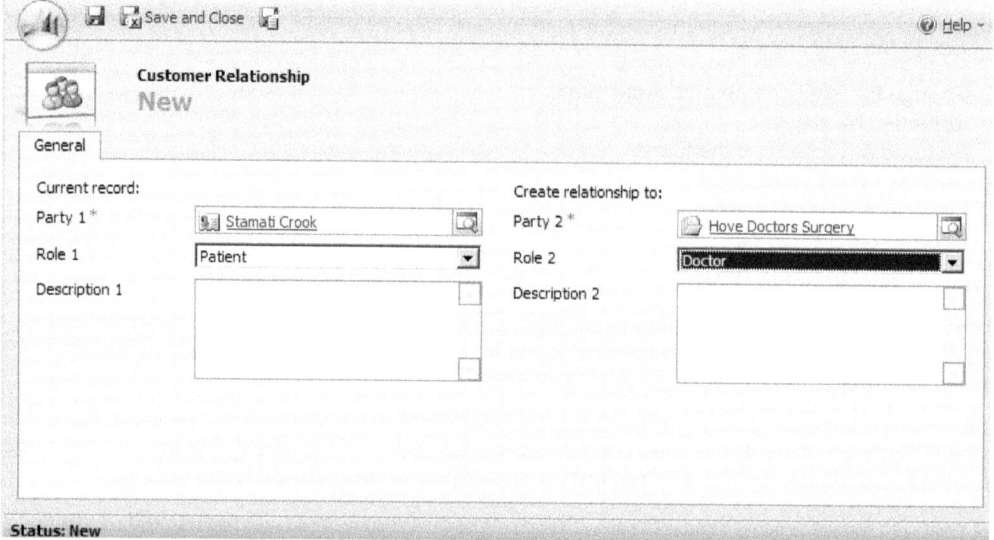

Note: Relationship Roles are flexible but are difficult to report on and difficult for new users to understand. A similar (but less flexible) relationship can be created between entities by creating relationships between entities.

19. Data Management

19.1. Export and Import from Excel

The simplest way to manage data is to create a view and export a spreadsheet from CRM with the additional fields required to allow data to be re-imported into CRM. The import process will update existing CRM records and also allow the creation of new ones.

See the section in the Using CRM chapter.

19.2. Bulk Import

An important feature of CRM is the ability to create new leads (assigned to a marketing list) quickly from a file of contact details received perhaps from a list vendor or a trade show.

The **bulk import** facility available from the **tools-import data** menu of the lead view (and for other entities) allows field mappings to be applied against the columns in the import file and for the data to be imported (specifying a marketing list allows easy tracking and deletion of the list in the future).

A **data map** needs to be made first to map the fields from the CSV file to the entity. The **settings-data management-data maps** area allows a data map to be imported from an XML file or created using a sample CSV file as a template (put the field names as the first line of the file).

Note: Dates must be in YYYY-MM-DD format.

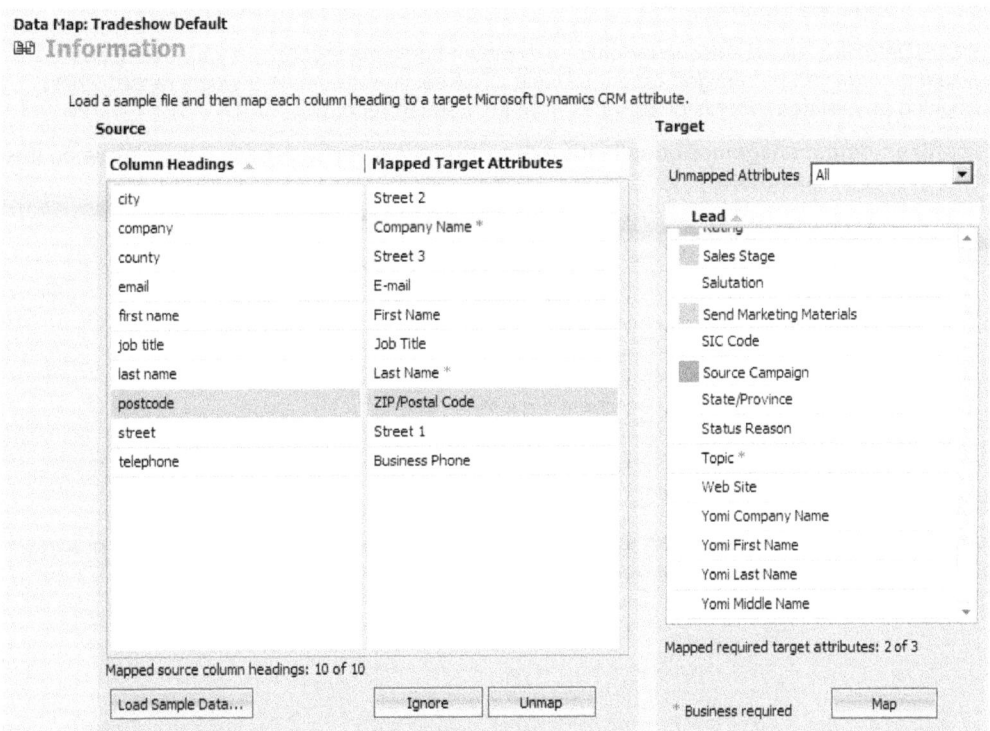

Required fields are highlighted with an asterisk and must all be specified before the data map can be used to import data from the **tools-import data** menu option of the entity. If you have selected any picklist fields for importing, you are asked to select corresponding mappings so that all imported records have the appropriate picklist values set automatically.

You are asked which entity and data map you want to use and whether duplicate records should be uploaded. A **system job** then begins and the file is processed in the background with all records allocated to the current user as the owner. System jobs can be viewed from the **workplace-system jobs** area.

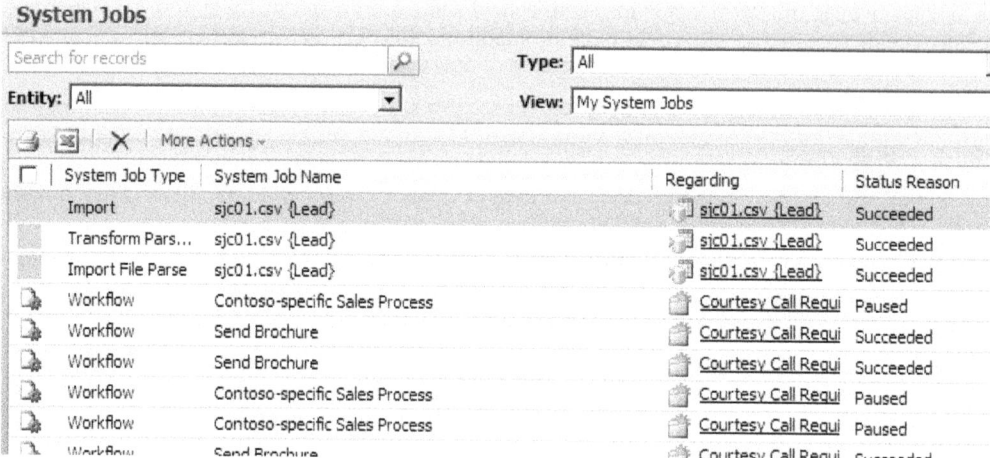

19.3. Duplicate Detection

Duplicate Detection allows rules to be defined to match duplicate records on various entities. Duplicate records can be **merged** (see the Using CRM section) to create a single record whilst reassigning any related records or activities from the deleted record.

The **settings-data management-duplication detection** area can be used to determine when the system checks for duplicates.

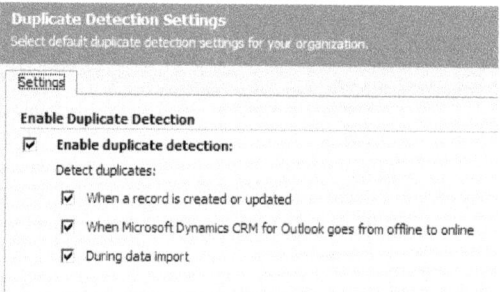

Alternatively, **duplication detection jobs** can be specified to regularly run the detection process (perhaps overnight) with the results displayed in the workplace-duplicates area.

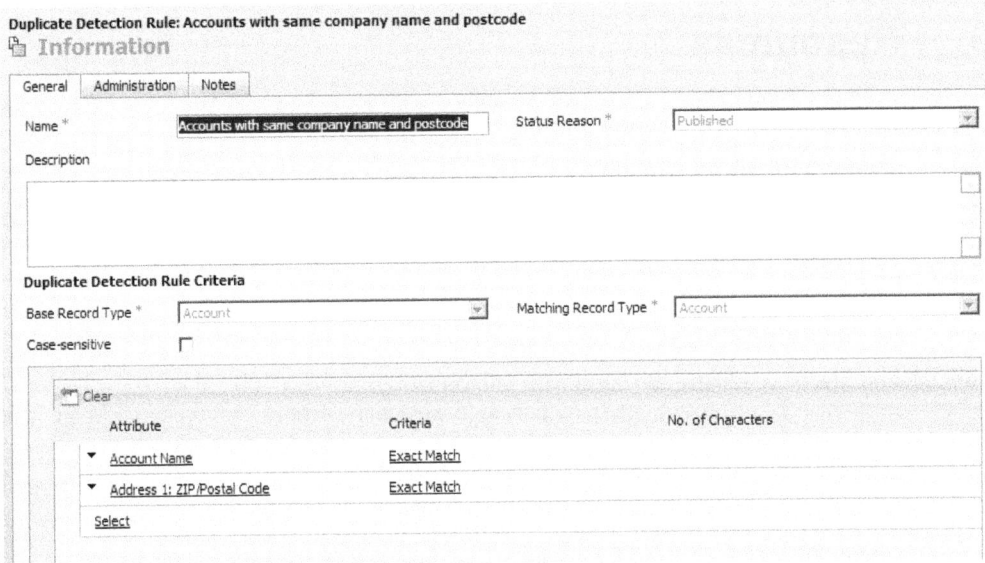

Duplicate Detection Rules can also be set up on various entities from the **settings-data management** area to help spot records that need to be merged.

19.4. Data Migration Manager

The data migration tool is designed to help with large migrations of data from one system to another. The main advantage is that related entities can be imported so, for example, each imported contact can create and be related to the corresponding account record. Greater control is possible over the data so that owners can be specified and note and attached files related to the main entity data.

A number of records can be deleted in the background using the Data Migration Tool and the **settings-data management-bulk deletion** area shows the progress of these jobs.

See the Microsoft documentation.

19.5. Third Party Software

Third party software is available to migrate data from other systems into CRM (see the Resources chapter) either when first installing the system or as a regular activity to synchronise accounting information for example.

20. Resources

Some resources are listed below. Please use the search engines to help you find more information and remember that the **resource center** provides access to many CRM resources.

20.1. Redware Research Limited

Redware Research Limited are the authors of this book, which is currently available online together with details of our software add-ons and other resources at http://www.redware.com/mscrm. Please take a look for updates and related information and please send us some feedback by email to sync@redware.com.

20.2. Recommended Books

Snyder, M. and Styger, J. (2006). **Working with Microsoft Dynamics CRM 3.0** Microsoft Press. This book is essential for all programmers beginning to work with CRM (a version for CRM 4.0 is due soon).

Your Working Day with Microsoft is a 60-page document available online from Microsoft. There is also a **surestep methodology** for partners to help project manage an implementation.

The **CRM Implementation Guide** is also available from Microsoft to help with planning an implementation.

20.3. Internet and Blogs

A small selection of bloggers are listed below. Search the internet for more Microsoft CRM Blogs:

- Simon Hutson - http://blogs.msdn.com/ukcrm/.
- Ronald Lemmen - http://www.ronaldlemmen.com/.
- Philip Richarsdson - http://philiprichardson.org/blog/.
- Jim Glass - http://blogs.msdn.com/jim_glass/default.aspx.
- Michael Hoehne - http://www.stunnware.com/crm2/.

20.4. Microsoft Training

Microsoft Training Partners offers various training courses. The Applications in Microsoft Dynamics 4.0 course probably covers much of what is in this handbook.

CRM 4.0 courses currently comprise:

- **8910 What is new in Microsoft Dynamics CRM 4.0** (1 day).
- **8913 Applications in Microsoft Dynamics CRM 4.0** (3 days).
- **8911 Installation and Deployment in Microsoft Dynamics CRM 4.0** (3 days).
- **8912 Customisation and Configuration in Microsoft Dynamics 4.0** (3 days).

These courses can lead up to Microsoft certification to become a **Microsoft CRM Certified Professional** (pass one exam only) or **Microsoft CRM Certified Master.**

We recommend F1 Computing Systems Limited (www.f1comp.co.uk) for training in the UK. Be careful when selecting several courses as some of the course material is repeated on different courses.

20.5. Third Party Software

A collection of CRM third party software is listed on this site - http://www.pimpmycrm.com.

http://www.c360.com

US company with several add-ons also reselling the mscrm-addons products.

http://www.redware.com

Developers of accounting integration, text messaging, credit checking and telephony applications (and publisher of this book).

http://www.mscrm-addons.com

Austrian developer of several utilities in Word mail merge, group calendar and telephony integration.

http://www.scribesoftware.com

Scribe offer upload and data migration solutions to load data (from Goldmine for example) into CRM and integrate with your own applications.

Telephony applications are also available for CRM from some vendors including Avaya, Cisco and LG.

21. Index

access mode 96
Account 29
ACT! 10
Activity 7, 31
   complete an activity 32
   convert to case 70
   converting to lead, opportunity, case 47
   create an activity 31
   fields 32
address 29
advanced find 20
alphabet bar 16
Announcements 47
application toolbar 16
Appointment 33
assign 27
Attachment 20
attributes
   customising 101
auto response 18
B2B 9, 29
B2C 9, 29
bulk deletion 110
bulk import 108
Business Closures 81
Business Unit 94
Calendar 45
Campaign 63
Campaign Activity 64
   distribute 66
Campaign Response 35, 66
   converting from lead 68
Campaign Template 66
Capacity .... *See* Service Type
Case 69
channel .... *See* Campaign Activity
company name field 9
Competitor 60
Contact 29
   primary 29
Contract 9, 72
   renewing 73
Contract Line Item 72
Contract Template 71
CRM
   Enterprise 11
   Professional 11
   Workgroup 11
CRM Live 12

currency 29, 59
Customer 9
   parent 29
customisation 8, 99
Data Migration Manager 12, 110
Discount List 50
Duplicate Detection 109
dynamic values
   email 24
   workflow 89
email 9, 33
   adding HTML 25
   attachments 9
   dynamic values 24
   Email Router 46
   knowledge base 23
   Knowledge Base article 70
   send direct email 25
   send email 23
   template 23
   templates 24
email router 12
Entity
   attributes 101
   customising 101
   mapping 104
   relationships 104
   renaming 106
Equipment 75
Excel
   export 21
   exporting and re-importing 108
Exchange Server 11
external connector 12
Facilities 75
fax 33
fiscal year 60
Form 17
   customising 103
   events 104
   IFRAME 104
   JavaScript 104
   toolbar 18
form assistant 19, 31
freight charges 57
Goldmine 10
history 32
Hosted CRM 11
iframe 104

Invoice
  status 59
JavaScript 103
Knowledge Base 73
  attaching into a Case 69
Leads 53
  convert lead 53
  qualify 54
Letter 9, 33
lookup window 18
mail merge 22
Marketing 15, 62
  planning task 64
Marketing List 62
  manage members 62
Microsoft Training 111
multi-tenancy 11, 94
My Work 45
navigation pane 16
Notes 17, 20, 69
Opportunity 9, 52, 54
  fields 54
  products 55
Order 58
  pricing 59
Outlook 7
  Calendar 7
  Task List 7
Outlook Client 36
  CRM Options 40
  CRM Toolbar 36
  Deleting Records 43
  Desktop Version 11
  Diagnostic Tool 43
  Laptop Version 7, 11, 12, 36
  mail merge 39
  Tasks 39
  tracking contacts 37
outsource vendor 67
paperclip 17
Phone Call 33
pipeline phase
  workflow 91
Preview Form 100
Price List Item 50
pricing method 50
Product 49, 52
  price list maintenance 9
  write-in products 57
programming 8
Programming CRM 8
Promote
  to response 66
Queue

assign activity 46
  in progress 47
quick campaign 26
Quick Campaign 63
quotas 60
Quotation 56
  activate 58
  printing 58
  revise 58
Redware Research Limited 111, 116
Relationship
  Mapping 106
relationship roles 106
relationship type 29
Report
  running a report 86
  SQL Server Reporting Services 87
Report Viewer 82
report wizard 82, 83
Report Wizard
  grouping 85
Reports 82
  scheduling 87
Resource 78
  preferred resources 80
  selection rules for service type 77
Resource Group 78
resources
  preferred by customer 80
Resources 15
Sales 15
  pipeline 91
  pipeline phases 52
  Sales Cycle 52
sales cycle 52
  pipeline 60
  quotas 60
  workflow 91
Sales Cycle
  pipeline 56
Sales Literature 60
Salesforce.com 10
Saleslogix 10
scheduling .... *See* Service Activity
Scheduling 75
security 8, 27
  SMTP Server 13
Security 94
Security Role 94, 97
Service 15
  calendar 34
Service Activity 35, 75
Service Calendar 81
Service Type 76

Microsoft CRM 4.0 User Handbook   115

Set Parent 37
Set Regarding 36, 39
Settings 15
sharing 27
Siebel 10
SQL Server 2005 11
Subject 60
synchronisation 37
   Emails 41
Synchronisation....................................... 42
   Address Book 43
   Deleting Records 43
   Laptop Client 43
   Tasks 39
TAPI 38
Task 32
Team 94, 97
Templates
   Word 23
Track in CRM 42
Unit Group 49
Unit Item 49
User 94, 95
user adoption issues 8

View
   actons 17
   customising 99
   export to Excel 21
   mail merge 22
   save 21
   toolbar 16
Virtual PC 13
web client 9
web services 12
Windows Workflow Foundation 88
Word 9
   mail merge 22, 63
   Templates 23
Workflow 9, 88
   pipeline phase 91
   steps 89
   triggers 88
   wait condition 90
   wait conditions 90
Workplace 15, 45
   calendar 34, 45
   personalise 47

22. redware research limited

redware research limited are the publishers of this book and we also offer consultancy and software add-ons for Microsoft CRM. Please look at http://www.redware.com/mscrm for more information.

Our software add-ons include:

- **Accounting Integration** to upload customers, products and invoices from various accounting packages into CRM.
- **Sales Cycle integration** to upload orders from CRM into the **Sage Line 50** accounting package.
- **SMS Text Messaging** via our own gateway integrated with the CRM phone call record.
- **Credit Checks** on all UK and Irish companies.
- **Telephony integration** with **TAPI** from the web application to integrate with your telephony and VOIP systems.

We are based on the south coast of England and offer **consultancy** and **troubleshooting** services for your CRM installation. We offer 5 and 10 day packages to help get your CRM project moving again if you are having problems with rollout and implementation and we work with training companies to help provide your users with the best training in all aspects of CRM.

We specialise in billing solutions and offer a 5 day **accounting integration** service where we take our existing software and integrate it with your accounting systems accessing the database directly from our code and creating invoices if possible with your software development kit.

Please call Stamati Crook on **+44 (0) 203 179 9444** with any consultancy or software enquiries or download and evaluate our software at http://www.redware.com/mscrm.

www.ingramcontent.com/pod-product-compliance
Ingram Content Group UK Ltd.
Pitfield, Milton Keynes, MK11 3LW, UK
UKHW051254180426
11947UKWH00020B/1715